Duquesne Studies

LANGUAGE AND LITERATURE SERIES

VOLUME TWENTY–TWO

John Donne's 1622 Gunpowder Plot Sermon

John Donne's 1622 Gunpowder Plot Sermon

A Parallel-Text Edition

*transcribed and edited
and with critical commentary
by Jeanne Shami*

Duquesne University Press
Pittsburgh, Pennsylvania

Published by

DUQUESNE UNIVERSITY PRESS
600 Forbes Avenue
Pittsburgh, Pennsylvania 15282–0101

Library of Congress Cataloging-in-Publication Data

Donne, John, 1572–1631.
    John Donne's 1622 Gunpowder Plot sermon: a parallel-text edition
/ by Jeanne Shami.
        p. cm.—(Language & literature series; volume 22)
    Includes bibliographical references and index.
    ISBN 0–8207–0261–7 (alk. paper).—ISBN 0–8207–0283–8 (pbk.:
alk. paper)
    1. Gunpowder Plot, 1605—Sermons. I. Shami, Jeanne. II. British
Library. Manuscript. Royal 17 B XX. III. Title. IV. Series:
Duquesne studies. Language and literature series; v. 22.
DA392.D66 1996
941.06′1—dc20   96–25367
                                       CIP

CONTENTS

PREFACE

The discovery and publication of MS Royal 17.B.XX, the only known autograph manuscript sermon by John Donne, has been a collaborative process from the very beginning. It began in the summer of 1992 with a visit to the British Library, and a decision to read manuscripts of unpublished, late Jacobean sermons. With only two days to spare for this preliminary research, I was unprepared for the news that I could not enter the Manuscripts Reading Room without the requisite letter of introduction from a "person of repute." At that moment, I had to decide whether to continue working with printed sermons in the North Library, or to acquire the necessary letter.

The crucial moment in the process of literary discovery was my decision to contemplate my dilemma over a half-pint of Brakspear's Special at the Museum Tavern across the street. I had all but given up on the manuscript reading plan, when I spied three colleagues walking toward the British Library. They joined me for a drink, I explained my predicament, and within minutes there was a solution. Acshah Guibbory and Julia Walker were not traveling with university stationery in their pockets, but Stella Revard coolly produced several sheets of Southern Illinois University letterhead from her handbag and wrote a letter of recommendation on the spot. Fortified and authorized, I was permitted entry to the Manuscripts Reading Room, and, within an hour, I had unearthed the first of three Donne manuscripts awaiting "discovery" in that archive.

Two colleagues from the University of Regina, Drs. Mary Blackstone and Cameron Louis, also happened to be reading in the Manuscripts Room that afternoon. They were able to discuss with me crucial matters of dating, provenance and paleography, and these were sufficient to encourage me to contact Dr. Peter Beal, manuscript expert for Sotheby's, and Dr. Hilton Kelliher of the Department of Western Manuscripts of the British Library. Both of these experts gave me valuable advice and encouragement at this stage of the process, and, of course, later.

Funding from the University of Regina's Faculty of Graduate Studies and Research enabled a return trip to the British Library in December 1992. My intention was to continue work on the new manuscript and to finish my preliminary search through the catalogue of sermons and miscellaneous theological tracts. I was heartened when I arrived to discover that Stella Revard was also working there (but this time, my pass was in order), and to discover, on the first day, a large miscellany of seventeenth century sermon tracts containing two more Donne sermons. The most significant discovery, however, took place only a few days before my return to Canada. A final run through the sermons index had produced one more manuscript I wanted to examine. This one turned out to be MS Royal 17.B.XX , the scribal copy of Donne's 1622 Gunpowder Anniversary sermon, corrected in his own hand. At the moment of discovery, I still didn't know what I had. In fact, it was only on the final day at the British Library that I recognized the careful corrections as Donne's, and realized that I had uncovered a manuscript that would alter the way we read seventeenth century sermons. I ordered a microfilm of the sermon, contacted Peter Beal from the airport departure lounge at Heathrow, and waited for his response. Several weeks later, I received his enthusiastic letter authenticating Donne's handwriting and urging me to publish an article immediately in *English Manuscript Studies*.

With three Donne manuscripts to deal with, one of them of unprecedented significance to scholars, I knew that I would have to enlist the help of experienced textual experts. I had already been in touch with Dr. Ernie Sullivan, one of the Donne *Variorum*'s textual editors, in the summer, and when I telephoned him to let him know what I had found, I expected to turn the matter over to him as the person most qualified to handle this material. Dr. Sullivan insisted, however, that I treat the material myself, adding that he would provide whatever help I needed. And he has remained true to his word. That I have produced this facsimile is largely due to his encouragement, patience and expertise. I have benefited at every stage of this process by our discussions, and by his willingness to explain and to demonstrate the principles and practice of textual scholarship. In addition, I am grateful for the opportunity that he provided for me to announce this discovery in an invited plenary address to the 1994 annual meeting of the John Donne Society.

The spirit of collaboration and support is the essence of the John Donne Society as I have experienced it. I would especially like to thank the following members, not only for their support for *this* project, but also for their interest in my ongoing research into Donne's sermons. For their help with textual matters, in particular, I thank Ernie Sullivan, Ted-Larry Pebworth, John T. Shawcross and Gary Stringer. I also want to acknowledge Dennis Flynn, Achsah Guibbory, Tom Hester, Dayton Haskin, Al Labriola, Meg Lota Brown, Paul Parrish and Camille Slights for their encouragement at crucial moments in this project's development.

At the University of Regina, I continue to find support and funding from the Faculties of Arts and Graduate Studies, particularly through the agency of Dean Murray Knuttila and Associate Vice-President (Research) Dr. Nick Cercone. I reserve special thanks for my colleague Dr. Cameron Louis, who has helped with innumerable details in editing this manuscript and who proofread my entire transcription before the edition went to press. Any errors that remain are mine, and will, no doubt, be noticed by the many reviewers who share in the collaborative process.

I have also received funding from the Bibliographical Society of America in timely support of this research. Their grant enabled a trip to the Folger Shakespeare Library to attend a workshop on "Editing After Poststructuralism" conducted by Dr. Paul Werstine. My thanks to the Folger Institute, Professor Werstine, Professor W. Speed Hill, and members of the seminar for their suggestions about how to deal most effectively with this material. At an important moment, Professor Wyman Herendeen also offered sound advice on the editing alternatives available to me.

To Professor Al Labriola and to Susan Wadsworth-Booth, Senior Editor for Duquesne University Press, I owe many debts of gratitude. They have been interested in publishing an edition of the Royal Manuscript from the moment of its discovery, and have done everything possible to bring the project to completion expeditiously without sacrificing excellence.

I am also grateful to the British Library for permission to produce a facsimile edition of MS Royal 17.B.XX, and for permission to quote from materials published in *English Manuscript Studies*.

Finally, to my husband Ken Mitchell, and to our children Andrew and Julia, I am grateful for the freedom and encouragement to travel whenever I need to, and for enthusiastic appreciation of whatever I accomplish. Their support marks the beginning and the end of the collaborative process.

John Donne's 1622
Gunpowder Plot Sermon

MS Royal 17.B.XX

Textual Scholarship and the Problem of Authorship

The British Library's MS Royal 17.B.XX was identified as a
scribal manuscript of a sermon by John Donne, corrected in his
hand, in December 1992. However, the discovery of an authorial
manuscript, particularly at this point in the history of textual
scholarship, creates as many problems as it solves. It introduces
the complication of an authorial presence into the textual status
of Donne's sermons at a time when scholars are being urged to
abandon both their fascination with the isolated author, and their
desire for a theory of origin that will explain textual difficulties
(De Grazia and Stallybrass 279). Consequently, the decision to
publish this manuscript in facsimile, to provide a complete transcription, and to list same-page verbal variants and complete
textual apparatus for comparison with the printed sermon text
from *Fifty Sermons*,[1] must be placed in the context of the cur-
rent debate in textual studies regarding "authors" and their "intentions." To what extent is the category of "author" important
for editing and interpreting this sermon? What textual issues are
raised by the discovery of a scribal manuscript of a sermon corrected in Donne's own hand?

This debate can be most clearly observed within the framework
of Shakespeare studies, where editors are challenging the as-
sumption that editorial problems would be simplified if scholars

---

[1] Until the discovery of MS Royal 17.B.XX, there was no known
manuscript source for this sermon. It appears in print as sermon XLIII
of *Fifty Sermons* (London, 1649), Potter and Simpson's copy-text for
their modern edition of the sermon.

could find the author's original manuscript. Paul Werstine, for one, has examined the categories that have proven indispensable to Shakespeare editors (i.e. author's foul papers, memorial reconstruction by actors, good and bad quartos, etc.) and shown how these have been produced, as he says, "by the desire for a certain kind of narrative, one which calls into being certain individuals—solitary author or lone actor—for the purpose of holding them solely responsible for the production of the most diverse phenomena" ("Narratives" 82). Jerome McGann is more emphatic: the stemmatic quest for a lost original, he argues, obscures "the true character of literary production" (*Critique* 74).

Furthermore, any treatment of an authorial manuscript must be seen in the context of the observation that, despite revolutionary developments in attitudes to textual editing (things such as the critical recognition of two authoritative *Lears*, the abandonment of eclectic texts, the acceptance of distinct historical versions of texts), textual editors still operate within the parameters of an author-centerd practice. They allow and even celebrate distinct versions of a work, but make an isolated author/reviser the controlling presence behind the author's texts (Werstine, "Textual Mystery"). As Foucault articulates the argument, these editors can handle difference if the differences can be termed authorial, and explicable by recourse to changing authorial intention (Foucault 111). Shillingsburg extends these observations, arguing that the editor can only recover the intention to *do* and not the intention to *mean* (36–37). How does this affect the way in which we perceive the relationship between MS Royal 17.B.XX and its first printed appearance in 1649 as Sermon XLIII in *Fifty Sermons* [hereafter cited as F50]?

In fact, this newly discovered authorial manuscript must be interpreted in the context of Jerome McGann's move away from the author-centerd scholarship of previous editors, and his contention that texts are *social* rather than *psychological* products. McGann's views have attracted a great deal of attention, particularly from those, like Janet Wolff, who understand the author as constituted in language, ideology and social relations. These scholars see the author as producing works that are not the product of intentions, final or otherwise, but of the material culture from which the author writes. As McGann argues, the standard for textual authority cannot rest with the author's intentions alone. This claim seems sensible, even with a manuscript corrected by the author. But even as we acknowledge the claims of competing authorities, we must resist choosing between a single author with clear intentions, or a socially constructed plurality of discourses. This manuscript discovery challenges us to expand our notion of the author by allowing the author to be non identical with a personal "self," to speak in a plurality of voices. And, paradoxically, this authorial manuscript challenges us to surrender the fiction that we can ever reconstruct what the author intended, if by that we mean what choices were self-consciously made and self-consciously effected. From the discovery of this manuscript, we can only *begin* to examine what Donne, the author, cared about, and what he was able to effect in manuscript and print forms.

To some extent, Foucault's explanation of the cultural significance of the "author-function" is pertinent here, for works require an "author" to have a certain cultural status (108–13). Nothing could be truer of this manuscript—it had lain for several centuries in miscellaneous limbo precisely because it had been unattributed. Nothing intrinsically meritorious in the work had been recognized prior to its identification as Donne's. Whatever its cultural status to this point, however, bringing Donne's history to bear on the manuscript allows us to see it more clearly as a particular sermon, embedded in the historical circumstances of its production in 1622, in the details of Donne's own developing career, and informed by other sermons Donne preached in the period, especially his sermon defending James's *Directions to Preachers* delivered at Paul's Cross on 15 September 1622, less than two months before (Shami, "Donne's Sermons" 394–95).

The questions raised when we compare Donne's corrected

manuscript and the version of the sermon printed in 1649 are problematic, to say the least. Many differences between the two sermons suggest that the version published in 1649 derives from Donne's revised holograph. This holograph, however, does not survive, making it very difficult to account intelligently for all the differences between the two versions. The situation is complicated by the fact that several of Donne's very careful insertions and deletions in MS Royal 17.B.XX disappear or are altered in the printed version. Editors may have opinions about which wording is more effective, but clearly it is dangerous to label "changes" as "improvements," just as it is dangerous to cling to Donne's original wording from the manuscript. In each case, the wording needs to be informed by as comprehensive and detailed a material context as possible. In a discussion of the editing of *Hamlet*, Werstine, for one, urges editors not to search for the indeterminable origins of variants, but to examine available sources "with a view to assessing the extent to which the two may be compatible or incompatible with one another" ("Textual Mystery" 2).

This edition contemplates the case discussed by Pebworth of a text, the witnesses of which radiate at different, indeterminate removes from a holograph. Pebworth uses the case of Donne's holograph verse letter, in which the editing corrects obvious errors and emends manuscript conventions to print ("Manuscript"). But the "authorial" sermon manuscript we now study, unlike Donne's holograph verse letter, cannot be so positive in the matter of accidentals. The degree to which the entire manuscript, as opposed to those specific places where Donne corrected the manuscript, can be said to be authorial is debatable. We simply have no way of knowing whether Donne read carefully, whether he intended every mark that appears on the manuscript leaves, or whether each leaf of the manuscript represents Donne's intentions for that time. Pebworth notes that the holograph verse letter follows older, freer conventions of capitalization, spelling and punctuation, while the printing tends to modernize all three.

This leads him to consider whether the copy-text for an edition of the verse letter can be chosen on the basis of accidentals alone, and to argue against the attempt because of the vast discrepancies between the two. He argues that the only rational choice for copy-text is on the basis of verbals. My argument is that both versions of this sermon are possible candidates for copy-text, because neither is verbally corrupt, although each shows different verbal choices. MS Royal 17.B.XX avoids certain scribal errors that appear in 1649, and is arguably very close to what Donne "intended" in November 1622. In addition, it provides readings that are logically and contextually superior to readings in the F50 version: "taken and neuer rescued" (line 1262) rather than "taken, and never returned" (F50, line 658); "all your extortions, and oppressions, and vsury, and bribery, and Simony" (lines 1412–13) rather than "all your extortions, and oppressions, and usury, and butchery, and simony" (F50, lines 733–34). However, F50 incorporates many of Donne's "revisions" as well as a host of differences that cannot clearly be defined as such. So while F50 represents a later stage in the textual history of this sermon, it also perpetuates and introduces errors not in the manuscript. The choice of either as copy-text is justifiable on different principles: MS Royal 17.B.XX in that it contains Donne's holograph insertions and corrections and provides correct readings for particular words; F50 in that it incorporates Donne's revisions and textual changes when he prepared the sermon for publication.[2]

For the editor, who must select a text according to a set of principles, and who must choose one word or one punctuation mark instead of another, the discovery of an authorial manuscript, therefore, creates dilemmas. In this particular case, choices must be made as to which version to privilege in the

---

[2] For an earlier discussion of related textual issues, see Pebworth and Sullivan, 1989.

presentation of the two available to us. My choice for editing this manuscript is to produce a documentary edition that will make available to readers, in as clear and accurate a form as possible, the data necessary for a complete study of the manuscript itself, as well as its relationship to the first printed version of the sermon in 1649 (F50). Consequently, this edition provides a facing-page facsimile and transcription of MS Royal 17.B.XX as the most visually dominant version. All substantive differences between the 1622 manuscript and the 1649 first edition are clearly indicated at the bottom of the page, in smaller type. I have made this choice knowing that the physical presentation of the data will not represent my view that both the manuscript and the printed version in *Fifty Sermons* comprise two distinct and equally important versions of the text. I also recognize that by foregrounding visually and spatially the authorially corrected manuscript rather than the probably authorial later printed version, I have distorted the significance of both versions. However, it does not seem practical or necessary to reproduce F50 as long as all variants which affect meaning are clearly indicated. More intensive comparative study will be based on comparison of the transcribed manuscript with the F50 version, readily available in full, in print and on microfilm.

The decision to produce a facsimile edition in the format described above is problematic but responds, I think, to the needs of readers. In the first place, the photographic reproduction of MS Royal 17.B.XX and the facing-page transcription fulfill the rationale of the documentary edition in "making more widely available scarce or unique texts whose inspection would otherwise necessitate a trip to a library" (W. Speed Hill, "Editing" 4). The uniqueness of the manuscript is not at issue; nor, one would hope, is the necessity of a careful transcription of the manuscript clearly distinguishing scribal and authorial corrections not apparent on microfilm. In addition, the decision to assist comparison by placing substantive variants at the bottom of the page is supported by the notion that MS Royal and F50 constitute distinct versions of the Gunpowder Plot sermon for 1622. The two texts are significantly altered to address different rhetorical situations, thus fulfilling Zeller's definition that a different version is characterized by a change in intentions and not simply by the quantity of variants (241). Some might argue that the laying out of both texts avoids the "editing" function, but the point of this volume is to provide the textual data for a thorough examination of the relations between these two versions: textual, rhetorical, political and other. McGann's assertion that textual criticism is a field of inquiry "that does not meet its fate in the completion of a text of an edition of a particular work" further encourages a presentation of the data so that different ends of textual criticism can be facilitated ("Monks" 187). W. Speed Hill's prediction that the day of eclectic texts has passed seems credible, as does his claim that the hegemony of establishing a text based on authorial intention now seems less persuasive in the face of the indeterminate text and the deconstructed author ("Editing" 23).

While this volume does not present a full narrative in which all textual materials are incorporated, then, it does provide the materials from which some of these stories might be written.

Bibliographical Description of MS Royal 17.B.XX

In the British Library's *Class Catalogue of MSS. Theology.* Vol. 14. (1). *Sermons and Treatises (Anglo-Saxon and English)*, p. 47, this sermon was catalogued simply as a sermon on Lamentations 4.20. The fuller entry in the *Catalogue of Western Manuscripts in the Old Royal and King's Collections* reads as follows: "Sermon on Lamentations iv.20, in commemoration of the King's deliverance from the Gunpowder plot. Beg. 'Of the Author of this book'. The preacher's name does not appear. Paper. ff.36. Quarto. 8 in. X 6 in. Circ. 1620–1625. Not in the old catalogues" (Warner and Gilson 230). The last statement means that the sermon is not part of the *Catalogus Librorum MSS. Bibliotechae Regiae* (1666) or of Edward Bernard's *Catalogi Librorum*

Manuscriptorum Angliae et Hiberniae in unum collecti (1697).
The manuscript is a single sermon, rebound in 1984 in morocco
half-binding and red cloth by the British Library. No information
is available about the manuscript's original binding, but in 1984,
the leaves were mounted on guards, and the sermon was rebound
with three other sermons in a miscellaneous collection of early
seventeenth century separates numbered MSS Royal 17.B.XVIII–
XXI. At that time, as well, certain leaves were repaired, and black
fly was inserted between each of the manuscripts. The sermon
is unsigned, does not have a title page, and is not mentioned in
Peter Beal's *Index of English Literary Manuscripts*.[3]

The manuscript, written primarily in secretary hand, appears
to be the work of one scribe. It is foliated in pencil in the upper
righthand corners (36 quarto leaves) by a later (probably nine-
teenth century) hand. At the very top righthand corner of the
first leaf, also in a later hand, is written in ink "17 B XX. p. 264.,"
indicating the page reference to this sermon in *A Catalogue of
the Manuscripts in the King's Library: An Appendix to the Catalogue of the Cottonian Library* by David Casley (1734). In darker
ink on almost every leaf, Donne himself has corrected copying
errors in the manuscript and filled in blank spaces, sometimes
between punctuation marks, left by the scribe. On the first three
leaves, proper nouns and, apparently, words that are to be emphasized, have been underlined, but this practice is discontinued
after the third leaf. The underlining appears to be contemporary
with the manuscript. It does not appear that the marks are
scribal, nor is there any evidence for attributing them to King
James, the supposed recipient of the manuscript. It is possible
that since the marks appear to be rhetorical rather than thematic
they are Donne's, and that they were intended to mark those
words meant to be italicized. In the end, however, it is virtually

---

[3] A preliminary discussion of this manuscript appeared in *English
Manuscript Studies* 5 (1994): 63–86.

impossible to recover the circumstances under which these marks were produced, to identify them in any way, or to interpret their significance.

The manuscript itself is written on one stock of unruled paper measuring 157mm. × 195mm. and bearing a watermark similar to Heawood 3499, a figure of two posts that Heawood dates "1617" from blank paper in the Phillipps Collection. The collation by watermarks is as follows: $1-7^4$, 8^1, 9^6 (the last leaf is an unfoliated strip attached to folio 30), 10^4, for a total of 38 leaves, the last two of which are blank. Several of the leaves have been recently repaired, but the manuscript is in good condition, and the text of the sermon is complete. There is some question as to whether the "Prayer before the Sermon," which precedes the Gunpowder Plot sermon in *Fifty Sermons*, formed part of this manuscript at one time, but the catalogue entry in the index to the Royal Manuscripts gives the number of leaves as 36, suggesting that for some time at least (i.e. since 1734, the date of Casley's *Catalogue*) the sermon has been transmitted in this form.

IMMEDIATE PROVENANCE AND TEXTUAL PRODUCTION

The concept of the author's intentions as it applies to the production of this manuscript in 1622 is a challenging one. Modern textual scholarship, following McGann, chooses to emphasize the author as a socially constructed being, and even an authorial manuscript as embedded in a plurality of discourses. Such an emphasis is not only possible with this manuscript, but extremely productive. To begin with, although this manuscript has lain unnoticed for 350 years, the sermon, in fact, is one about which we know a great deal. As F50 informs us, the sermon was scheduled to be preached by Donne at Paul's Cross, 5 November 1622, on the anniversary of the Gunpowder Treason, but was delivered inside the Cathedral on account of bad weather. Donne chose as his text Lamentations 4.20: "The breath of our Nostrills, the Anointed of the Lord was taken in their pitts." And, in a letter of 1 December 1622, addressed to Sir Thomas Roe, English Ambassador at Constantinople, Donne alludes specifically to this sermon. With the letter, Donne apparently sent a copy of his first published sermon, which had been delivered earlier that year at Paul's Cross (15 September 1622), defending King James I's *Directions to Preachers* (issued on 4 August). The letter to Roe reports that the 15 September sermon had been preached to address the concerns of many persons who had been scandalized by the proposals to marry Prince Charles to the Spanish Infanta, and who had "admitted suspicions of a tepidnes in very high places" as a result of the new restrictions on preaching. Donne compares this sermon with the Gunpowder Anniversary sermon, commenting that on 5 November he was "left more to [his] owne liberty." He continues:

> and therfore I would I could also send your Lordship a Copy of that; but that one, which, also by commandement I did write after the preachinge, is as yet in his Majesties hand, and, I know not whether he will in it, as he did in the other, after his readinge thereof, command it to be printed; and, whilst it is in that suspence, I know your Lordship would call it Indiscretion, to send out any copy thereof; neither truly, ame I able to committ that fault; for I have no Copy.[4]

However, King James did not, in fact, order the sermon printed, and the sermon manuscript seems to have remained "in that suspence" until now. MS Royal 17.B.XX is a fair copy by a scribe evidently working directly from Donne's own holograph manuscript, and under Donne's supervision. The manuscript has been corrected by Donne and is apparently that very copy the King commanded—and which has remained unrecognized and uncatalogued as Donne's, in the Royal Manuscripts collection.

---

[4] SP 14/134/59. Potter and Simpson 4.35.

The reference to the sermon "which I did write after the preach-inge" that is now with the King need not be taken literally (i.e. it is not necessary to conclude that it refers to Donne's original holograph, no longer extant). Donne's statement likely refers to the entire process by which the sermon as delivered orally was produced in written form (i.e. a holograph by Donne, written out in full after the sermon was delivered; a scribal copy taken from this holograph and corrected by Donne). This interpretation en-compasses both meanings of "write," i.e. to compose, and to write out in full or amplify, and is consistent with what we know about Donne's practice of sermon transmission. Since it was customary for Donne to preach only from notes, such a "writ-ing" would have been necessary once the King had commanded the sermon.[5] The word "write" could also encompass the scribal "writing out" (perhaps from Donne's own abbreviated manu-script), especially since the manuscript was clearly produced under Donne's supervision. Similarly, the statement to Roe that "I have no copy" makes sense if it is taken literally to mean that he has his own original manuscript, but he has no extra copy. The only copy (corrected by him) is in the hands of the King, and Donne stresses the indiscretion of proliferating copies before he is sure what James's intentions are with regard to the sermon.

The provenance of the manuscript as it emerges in Donne's letter to Roe with its hesitancy, its obscurity about how many copies exist, and its reluctance to specify how this copy relates to the one mentioned in the letter, confirms our sense of this manuscript as a socially constructed text. The sermon was not published in Donne's lifetime, however, and it is conceivable and likely that Donne's language in the letter to Roe is deliber-ately ambiguous, and results from Donne's awareness of the

---

[5] John Sparrow, "John Donne and Contemporary Preachers: Their Preparation of Sermons for Delivery and for Publication," *Essays and Studies by Members of the English Association* 16 (1930): 145–78.

indiscretion of circulating a sermon which was being examined, for whatever reasons, by the King.[6] These indirections are taken up in more detail in considering Donne's subsequent changes to the text of the sermon for publication in F50, but already we are required to be aware of the material realities within which this sermon was created and disseminated.

Donne's Corrections

Donne's holograph corrections reveal more than we have hitherto known about his process of preparing a sermon for distribution after he had delivered it orally. It appears that Donne produced an original manuscript, in his own hand, either before he delivered the sermon, or more likely afterward when it was commanded by the King. Donne then had a scribe copy from his own holograph; at times the scribe is unable to decipher Donne's words (usually those in Latin or Hebrew, but sometimes in English) and leaves a blank space. The scribe then goes through the sermon again (or perhaps parts of it) and tries to fill in those passages he omitted the first time through; we see this on folio 8, where he has left insufficient space for a Latin quotation and has to crowd the final two words. This also appears to be the case on lines 196–97 (state, That forme of gouer = ment), line 1432 (exclamation), and line 1452 (Tutelar), to cite several more obvious examples. It is possible that after filling in the blank spaces the scribe trimmed the pages and then reread one more time, correcting any errors. This possibility is suggested by the fact that on folio 33v the marginal reference to 2.reg.23, which has been partially cropped, has been corrected by putting the 2 above the other words. There is also the possibility that several marginal and interlinear dots, not decipherable as punctuation marks,

---

[6] The importance of discretion for Donne is discussed in Shami, "Donne on Discretion."

provide a cue for either the scribe or Donne (or both) that corrections or additions are needed. Examples of these occur near lines 84, 312, 546, 629, 653, 674, 939, 985, 1226, 1432 and 1509, although it is impossible to determine a clear pattern to such marks.

In general, one can see that the scribe copies more quickly as he goes along. The hand becomes looser as the sermon proceeds, and there are more scribal errors and corrections in the scribal hand toward the end. In addition, the scribe apparently experiences more difficulty in deciphering Donne's script as he goes along. Most of the long blank spaces filled in by Donne occur in the latter half of the manuscript, suggesting that Donne's own script, too, may have become more hurried as the sermon progressed. The manuscript appears to have been prepared in haste, explicable in the context of the King's demand to see the sermon, which was preached on 5 November and was in the King's hands no later than 1 December when Donne wrote to Roe.

When the scribe had completed his transcription and corrections, Donne apparently proofread and corrected the manuscript himself. He added letters, changed words, perhaps punctuated, and filled in blank spaces left by the scribe (who invariably left more room than Donne needed because Donne's script was more compact). There is no evidence, except possibly the underlining, that Donne went over the manuscript more than once. In places such as line 1152, where the scribe has left too much room, Donne fills the extra space with a tilde. The corrections also reveal the precision and care with which Donne attended to the delivery of a copy of his sermon to the King. Donne not only corrected obvious scribal errors that obscured sense but took care to ensure that particular words were also "accurate." This included making changes from "the" to "that" (lines 493, 1035) and "hath" to "had" (line 806), where either would make sense. In at least one instance (line 1180), Donne has corrected the spelling of a word (from "derected" to "directed"), suggesting that Donne was more precise in matters of spelling (to the point of marring the appearance of the leaf for a one-letter correction) than was normal for this period when spelling was various and inconsistent (Baugh and Cable 203–09). In addition, it is possible that Donne actually corrected or added punctuation (the colon on line 286, the change from a comma to a semicolon with the addition of a period on line 345) as he proofread.

Many of Donne's characteristic orthographic habits noted by Croft, Petti and Barker can be observed in the corrections to sermon MS Royal 17.B.XX. Donne's corrections are revealed in the characteristic traces of his neat italic hand. The most obvious example in this manuscript occurs at lines 1533–34, where Donne fills the space with "mercy and benignity, to let him out." His epsilon *e* (which leans slightly backward and appears to rise slightly above the general level of other letters), alternate italic *e*, and curled-back *d* are unmistakable. At other times Donne writes single words in his neatest but still usually very distinctive script, and even inks over, in his darker ink, one or two letters of the scribe to make them clearer (such as the very first word: "Lamentati").

A distinguishing feature of Donne's style is that many of his letters appear in two or three forms, especially *y*, *d*, *t*, *f* and *e*. The manuscript provides numerous examples that conform to the types identified by Croft and Petti. For example, Petti notes that Donne's hand demonstrates at least three varieties of *y*. Two of these can be clearly seen on folio 36: the first is the one Petti describes with a tail ending in a little curl to the left, illustrated at line 1533 (mer*cy*). Line 1533 also has the *y* ending in a loop crossing the tail (benignit*y*).

While Donne uses several *e*'s, the epsilon *e* is perhaps his most characteristic form and is frequently used in this manuscript: line 1533 (m*e*rcy, b*e*nignity), lines 796–97 (th*e*, anoint*e*d, Br*e*ath), line 802 (insinuat*e*), and line 1534 (l*e*t).

Petti also notes that Donne characteristically leaves the top of the *o* open. An example of this formation occurs at line 1534.

Various forms of Donne's *s* are also characteristic. One form appears clearly, for example, at line 797 (*s*piritus, no*s*trills). Another form of *s*, best represented by line 1152 (vi*s*ion) is identical to the form of *s* seen in the verse letter holograph, line 16 (vertuou*s*).

Donne's *h* also appears to be characteristic in this manuscript. It has a straight ascender and a narrow shoulder widening out to a broader base. It is best represented in lines 400–01 (now*h*ere), and line 1534 (*h*im).

The word "directed" on line 1180 provides an excellent opportunity to observe similarities between this word and the same word in line 5 of the verse letter holograph.[7] Both have the same long upright ascender on *d*; the *i* in the manuscript is more upright than in the verse letter, but there is the same break after the *i* before the *r* begins; the sermon has the same *r* with high ligature to epsilon *e*; the *c* is very similar; the *t* in the sermon is not the same as in the verse letter, i.e. the cross-bar on the poem is not a separate stroke. The epsilon *e* leading to a curled-back *d* in the sermon is identical to the epsilon *e* leading to straight ascender *d* of the poem, but the *d* of the sermon is one of the most characteristic of Donne's letters. On the whole, the similarities are remarkable, and the variations are ones that have many other precedents in Donne's writing.

But while there is no mistaking Donne's hand in this manuscript, and while it is possible to compile tables of corrections that are definitely, probably and possibly by Donne, it is difficult to interpret the meaning and significance of his corrections. Nor can every mark he has made carry an absolutely positive value. Despite the indications of thorough proofreading noted above, for example, Donne the corrector or proofreader (as opposed to Donne the author) clearly missed several errors and even introduced at least one error into the manuscript. On three occasions,

---

[7] The features of this holograph poem are debated in Gardner (1972) and Barker (1973).

Donne fails to add words to the top of a leaf, which were the catchwords at the bottom of the previous leaf (lines 864, 1039, 1284). Nor does he correct other errors involving catchwords: on one occasion, the catchword "are" is offered for "our" (line 81); on one occasion, the scribe indicates "gaine" as the catchword (line 581) when the word is "againe" (line 582). On two occasions (line 334 and line 1013), the word "there" is mistakenly used for "their," and this despite the fact that in the manuscript several scribal corrections indicate that both Donne and the scribe distinguished between the two forms (e.g., lines 344, 881, 932). The word "his" is repeated at line 1082, although normally words carelessly written twice are deleted (line 883). In addition, Donne allows the clearly mistaken "them" to remain for "then" at line 73.

Most of these errors are not remarkable, and can be explained as normal proofreader's errors. More puzzling is Donne's failure to correct the phrase "in *foueis*, in pitts" at line 1279. From the paragraph as a whole, and from the marginal annotation at that point, it is clear that the phrase should be in the singular, i.e. "in *fouea*, in a pit," in order to allow for the contrast with the plural form later in the paragraph. The error is corrected in F50. A correction in this particular place in the manuscript would have been possible, though messy. Are we to conclude that Donne didn't notice the problem, that he didn't consider it important, that he didn't know how to correct it neatly, or that he did not read each leaf with equal care? There are no other authorial corrections on folio 30, which is near the end of the manuscript, so it is possible that Donne was cutting corners by the time he got to this stage in the correction process. But we cannot be certain.

Another curious "correction" is Donne's insertion of the word "especially" at the end of a phrase at line 918, thus creating what, to modern ears at least, is an awkward and redundant sentence: "They are our breath; our breath is theyrs, in good interpretations of their actions, and it is theirs especially in our prayers to allmightie god for them especially." There seems to be no stylistic reason why Donne would add the second "especially," and yet an editor would have to make a difficult choice in excluding a word Donne had so carefully added. In F50, the second "especially" is omitted.

Donne's own corrections tell us much about his methods of composition in preparing this manuscript for presentation to King James I. But they clearly create as many problems of interpretation as they resolve. If we judge all of Donne's marks on the manuscript to be "intentional," we still must distinguish, if we can, between intention to *mean* (which is difficult to recover) and intention to *do*. While *intention to do* appears more straightforward, it is still not something about which we can be certain. And Donne's intentions regarding corrections *not* made are even more difficult to recover. Paradoxically, many of these intentions can only be discerned through comparison with the later, published version of this manuscript, despite the fact that the physical marks of his hand are not evident there.

TRANSMISSION

Contemporary

As we have noted, this sermon was delivered, at St. Paul's on 5 November 1622, presumably from Donne's notes. When it was commanded by the King soon after, Donne presumably wrote out his notes in full, had them copied by a scribe, proofread and corrected the scribe's copy, and delivered the manuscript to King James. On 1 December 1622, Donne indicated to Sir Thomas Roe that he did not have a copy of this sermon in his possession. Donne's letter to Roe indicates that he also sent a copy of his first published sermon to Roe; it was not unusual for Donne to distribute copies of his sermons to his friends. A letter to Henry Goodyer, 30 August 1621, for example, begins with Donne's apology for not having written out a sermon which Goodyer had requested; he reveals that a pain in his right wrist has made writing impossible for three weeks (Donne, *Letters* 154–59).

Seventeenth Century

Donne died in 1631, leaving revised sermon manuscripts with his executors Henry King and Dr. Montford. The version of this sermon published in F50 (1649) is substantively different from that in MS Royal 17.B.XX, but I will argue that the differences are authorial. It appears that both the Royal MS and the F50 version derive from an original holograph source, presumably that written out immediately after delivery of the sermon. *Fifty Sermons* was intended as a companion volume to *LXXX Sermons*; both were licensed in 1639–40 and entered in the Stationers' Register. John Donne Jr. dedicated the volume to his patron, the Earl of Denbigh, stressing Denbigh's education in Venetian (i.e. republican) principles of government and his stewardship in the learning of Padua. At the same time, he warns that the religion embodied in his father's sermons must not be expunged by a "fiery zeale in succeeding ages" (F50 sig. A2v). In fact, though the sermons were entered at Stationers' Hall in 1644, the younger Donne delayed publication for fear of persecution by the Commonwealth government, on the one hand, and perhaps in reaction to a reluctance on the part of ecclesiastical authorities, on the other. Donne Jr. said he had "many disputes" with these authorities over statements his father had been able to make in public pulpits, without dispute, during his lifetime (Bald 576). By 1734, as we have seen, this sermon was bound with three other sermons, noted by Casley in his Catalogue, numbered MSS Royal 17.B.XVIII–XXI. XVIII is a translation of Basil's homily on Deuteronomy 15, dedicated to the Duchess of Summerside, by Mildrid Cicill. XIX is James Cleland's sermon on the Gowry Conspiracy, preached at Canterbury Cathedral, 5 August 1616. The final sermon, XXI, is "A Description of the sone of God according to his harmonie, relation conformitie & union with the father." Though unattributed, the sermon is dedicated to James I.

Henry Alford

After the seventeenth century, the sermons were not edited again until Henry Alford undertook the project and published a six-volume edition of Donne's works in 1839. Encouraged by his own reading and by Coleridge's view that the re-publication of these works was necessary, Alford proposed an edition that would offer a selection from the *Sermons*, not to exceed four octavo volumes. At the same time, Alford decided to omit "one or two passages containing allusions, common at the time when they were delivered, but likely to offend [his] modern readers" (1.vi).[8] Subsequently, the decision was made to republish all of Donne's sermons, and from this point Alford "adhered scrupulously" to Donne's text, offering the sermons to his readers in their "original unmutilated form" (1.vi). Alford's edition of the 1622 Gunpowder Plot sermon was based on the version printed in *Fifty Sermons*. This was not one of the sermons from which Alford excised passages deemed unsuitable for his Victorian readers, although he did modernize spelling and punctuation, and offered emended readings for some words. In assessing Alford's edition, I concur with Donne's modern editors, George Potter and Evelyn Simpson, who judge the text of this edition to be, given his decision to modernize, "reasonably careful," and who note that "frequently (though not always) his [Alford's] emendations and the material in his footnotes are intelligent and valuable" (1.29). Because Alford frequently does not acknowledge emendations, and because he modernizes punctuation, spelling and italicization, the text is of little scholarly use to readers interested in these particulars, but it is difficult to underestimate the historical significance of Alford's edition.

---

[8] See Haskin (1992) for a discussion of Alford's edition in the context of Donne's Christmas sermons.

George Potter and Evelyn Simpson

Potter and Simpson's edition of Donne's sermons was based primarily on the three folio editions of the seventeenth century, but supplemented where possible with information from earlier editions and manuscript sources. When Potter and Simpson produced their edition of Donne's sermons (1953–62), they were aware of only six manuscripts dating from Donne's lifetime, copied by other hands.[9] A seventh became available in 1954, and was treated in an appendix to volume 2 of the *Sermons* (365–71). These sources cast light on only 16 out of 160 of Donne's sermons. There was no manuscript source for the sermon on Lamentations 4.20 when it was edited.

Since 1992, three more manuscripts containing sermons by Donne have come to light. The first of these is MS Royal 17.B.XX. The second is a manuscript containing five sermons, all by Donne, written in several professional secretary hands and certainly predating the earliest printed versions of these sermons. Of the sermons in this collection, the three preached at marriages exist in other manuscript copies. However, the two remaining sermons do not exist in any other manuscript form. The third manuscript contains two sermons by Donne amidst a variety of miscellaneous tracts of the seventeenth century. These two sermons (on Ecclesiastes 12.1 and Matthew 21.44) are the two most frequently copied of Donne's sermons and were important in establishing editorial principles for Potter and Simpson's modern edition of Donne's *Sermons*. This raises to 19 the total of Donne's sermons for which we possess manuscript sources.[10]

Study of existing sources led Potter and Simpson to conclude that the texts of sermons in F80 and F50 (the two folios that concern us) came from a fairly uniform manuscript source, different

---

[9] Readers are directed to the General Introductions, "On the Manuscripts" and "On the Text" in Potter and Simpson's edition (1.33–82).

[10] These sermons are currently being examined by Jeanne Shami.

from and later than the primary source manuscripts from which existing manuscripts had been copied. Some of the sermons in F80 and F50 were considerably revised by Donne, others not changed from their earlier, manuscript forms. According to Potter and Simpson, Donne presumably went over all the manuscripts for the sermons in these folios late in life, "some perhaps written out in full for the first time then, some revised extensively, some slightly, and some left unchanged." Accordingly, in choosing their text, they saw it as "obviously necessary" to follow the author's own revised wording, evidenced in the folio editions. In their view, these editions "contain Donne's sermons in the revised form in which he wished that they should be given to the world" (1.46).

Donne's sermon on Lamentations 4.20 was not edited until 1959. Potter and Simpson had only F50 as their copy-text, supplemented by suggested emendations from Alford. In their edition, Potter and Simpson correct several of F50's obvious errors: "Chuches" for "Churches" in F50 line 797, "Thai" for "That" in line 638, "rest" for "rests" in line 471, "Hope" for "Pope" in line 220, "have" for "gave" in line 134, "dispute now" for "dispute not now" in lines 68–69, "Concubins" for "Concubin" in line 452, "righteousnessc" for "righteousnesse" in line 728. None of these errors appears in MS Royal 17.B.XX.

The wide variations in spelling, capitals, italics and punctuation in their sources did not leave Potter and Simpson confident that they could determine Donne's own practice. They argued that one could get close to Donne's own practice in the earliest editions, but acknowledged that the Folios could contain revisions by Donne. With this in mind, they decided to follow the Folio text where it existed as their basic text version. They corrected passages only where the basic text was wrong "on its own principles," although it is unclear from either their theory or practice what these principles might be or how they might affect editorial choices. Many changes made by Potter and Simpson to the F50 version in matters of punctuation and italics appear arbitrary, especially the insertion of a comma after "Kingdome" at F50 line 78, the comma after "kingdom" on F50 line 209 and the italicizations at F50 lines 454, 521, 553. Potter and Simpson comment that there is considerable variation between conventions of punctuation, capitalization and italicization in the printed versions when compared with early manuscripts. It seems arbitrary, then, to select three or four places in which to intervene among numerous opportunities.

Emendations by Potter and Simpson to marginal Biblical references succeed in correcting errors, but it is significant that in three cases the Royal MS agrees with F50 in offering the incorrect version (Job 30.1 rather than Job 30.8, 9; Genesis 28.18 rather than Genesis 28.17; Judges 9.8 rather than Judges 9.14, 15). The presence of these common errors suggests that F50 was copying faithfully from its (authorial) source in printing its text. These common errors also correct, to some extent, Potter and Simpson's claims that the compositor of F50 was careless; perhaps the presumption that Donne always quotes accurately from his Biblical and patristic sources needs to be qualified once more by D. C. Allen's observations made some years ago about the varying degree of accuracy in Donne's use of Biblical quotations.[11]

COMPARISON WITH SERMON XLIII IN *FIFTY SERMONS*

The question of authorial intention as it relates to Donne's apparent revisions of his manuscript for publication is crucial to further textual and interpretive decisions. The standard edited text for this sermon differs significantly from the version preserved in the Royal Manuscript. What is the relationship be-

---

[11] In addition to Allen's article, see the comments on Donne's marginal annotations to *Biathanatos* in Ernest W. Sullivan II's edition (xxxvii–xxxviii).

tween these two versions of the sermon, and to what extent do the differences between the Royal manuscript and the first printed version of the sermon indicate authorial revision? Potter and Simpson argued that F50 came from a primary source containing moderate though not radical revisions by Donne himself. They also thought it probable that the sermons in that volume came from manuscript copy of the same excellence as that from which the 1640 folio was printed, although more carelessly typeset and proofread. Consequently, Potter and Simpson used F50 as their copy-text, emending what they took to be obvious copyists' errors in marginalia, punctuation and italics.

A collation of MS Royal 17.B.XX with F50 does support Potter and Simpson's view that F50 is derived from an authorial manuscript. One of the most interesting textual connections between the Royal MS and F50 is signalled by F50's "now no where" [202–03] (which seems to combine the "now here" mistake of Donne's scribe at lines 400–01, with Donne's correction to "nowhere" in 1622). It is possible that the manuscript from which the text for F50 was taken created the same difficulty as this one (i.e. the scribe mistook "nowhere" for "now here"). Then Donne, or someone else, corrected the error, probably interlining "nowhere" above "here" as a correction for the printer (thus leaving the "now" intact). Whatever scenario is posited to explain this curious wording, this common error between the two versions of the sermon (as with the common marginal errors) suggests that F50 is also derived from an authorial source. So, too, does the presence of "transportition" (F50 line 199) and "transportion" (MS 392) for "transportation" (Alford, Potter and Simpson [line 244]).

On the basis of the differences between the two versions, it seems plausible to argue, as do Potter and Simpson, that, on the whole, the changes in F50 represent "deliberate and intelligent" (1.46) revisions to the manuscript copy Donne had of this sermon, and that the revisions are significant enough to constitute a second "version" of this sermon. Many of the qualifications, clarifications and rhetorical amplifications are changes that show the shift from oral to written delivery. Other rewordings translate a phrase, alter the syntax (sometimes moving from a more to a less dramatic mode suitable for print), alter rhetorical emphasis, change the diction, eliminate words. Many of these changes also show a shift in politics.[12] There is no denying that such data is problematic. One hesitates, for example, to use the word "improvement" to describe differences. But the differences do suggest that Donne was involved with the rewordings. Whether one posits a change in decorum (oral to written), a greater concern for distinguishing between political responsibilities of both the King and his counselors, shifts in emphasis from one occasion to the other, desire to avoid misunderstandings, or concern for greater clarity or precision, many of the differences between the MS and F50 support the view that many of the changes (the majority, in fact) are authorial. However, positing two authorial versions of the same work raises the question of whether an editor is wise invariably to prefer a later, revised version to an earlier one—particularly when that earlier version is corrected in Donne's hand and presumably is in the form he wished it to be in late November 1622, close to the moment of its creation and delivery, though not when he was revising it for publication.

The differences between MS Royal 17.B.XX and F50 fall into four main categories: significant changes in content, substantive rewordings, stylistic rewordings and innumerable changes in spelling, punctuation and italics (which may or may not be authorial). The first two of these, in particular, support the argument that the differences are "authorial" and "intentional," at

---

[12] See works cited by Norbrook; Gray and Shami; Shami ("Kings," "Introduction," "Donne's Sermons"); Patterson ("John Donne, Kingsman?", "All Donne," "Misinterpretable Donne"); Brown; Harland on reevaluations of Donne's politics.

least in the context of the early Caroline years before 1631, when Donne might have revised and amplified his sermon. A discussion of the first of these helps to reconstruct Donne's political intentions with regard to this sermon in both its forms.

Four sections in particular were added or significantly revised and indicate more clearly both Donne's political intentions in his earlier version, and what he cautiously refrained from spelling out at the time of delivery.

"The Prayer Before the Sermon"

The printed version contains "The Prayer Before the Sermon," but this is not part of the sermon manuscript as we have it. This prayer, however, is important in that it provides a context within which readers may interpret the content of the sermon, and fulfills the Canon of the Church that required prayer before each sermon.[13] In the prayer, Donne offers thanks and praise for the nation's providential deliverance from a Catholic plot, and he encourages continued vigilance against Catholics. Deliverance from the Gunpowder Plot continued to be celebrated annually in churches across England. However, in the *Directions for Preachers* issued 4 August 1622, King James had specifically instructed preachers to curtail their anti-Papist commentary.[14] Burgin and Wall argue that in this sermon Donne shifted his emphasis in his treatment of the Plot from its religious to its political dimensions, carefully limiting his attack "only to those few Catholics who actually took part in the Plot" (23). Such a move would allow him to engage in limited anti-Catholic invective,

---

[13] Canon LV of the 1603 *Constitutions and Canons Ecclesiastical* (Wing 4100) required prayer before sermons, lectures and homilies, and outlined specifically the nature and even the wording of the prayer.

[14] These *Directions* and several accompanying documents are reproduced in Kenneth Fincham's *Visitation Articles and Injunctions of the Early Stuart Church* (211–15).

while still implicating those who opposed James's *Directions* and his pro-Spanish foreign policy in the rebellion against authority represented in the Gunpowder Plot. In this prayer, however, Donne unequivocally lays the "only ground of the Treason of this day" upon "that [Catholic] Religion." In addition, Donne states specifically that the commemoration of the Plot at the universities rightly involves a "detestation of their Doctrines [not their persons], that plotted this" (Potter and Simpson 4.235). The Prayer stresses the true catholicity of the Churches of England, Scotland and Ireland as opposed to the plotters "who pretend themselves the onely sonnes thereof" (4.236), and prays for the enlargement of God's mercies on the political and religious institutions of the kingdom: the Church, the King, the Prince, the Privy Council, the Clergy, the Houses of Commons and Lords, the Universities. In particular, he prays that all of the preaching and government of the clergy in their several jurisdictions be focused on preventing "all reentrances of that [Catholic] religion." Donne's anti-Catholic statements are clear and direct: that they politicize the doctrines of the Papists should not obscure Donne's unequivocal rejection of that religion, and not simply of the Gunpowder plotters themselves. Such comments prepare the ground for the entire sermon, and throw into relief Donne's clear rejection of the political aspirations of the plotters.

Samuel and the Jews

> you said to me says *Samuel, 1 Samuel 12.12.* Nay
> but a king shall ræigne over vs,
> (MS Royal, lines 340–42)

> You said to mee (says *Samuel,* by way of Reproofe
> and Increpation) *You said, Nay but a King shall
> reigne over us;* Now, that was not their fault; but
> that which followes, The unseasonablesse and
> inconsideration of their clamorous Petition, *You
> said a King shall reigne over us,*
> (F50, lines 170–73)

These lines constitute an important addition of material. Donne wants to clarify the way in which Samuel and the Jews could legitimately expostulate with God. Donne distinguishes between Samuel's authorized function of "Reproofe and Increpation" (the proper behaviour of a prophet, which Donne outlines elsewhere) and the unseasonableness and inconsideration of the clamourous petition of the Jews. Donne had argued the same point in a sermon preached at the Hague, 19 December 1619, but revised in 1630. There he said that though prophets could "chide the Kings openly, and threaten the Kings publiquely, and proclaime the fault of the Kings in the eares of the people confidently, authoritatively" (2.303) it was seditious and impertinent to argue that "therefore the Minister may and must do" (2.303). And if such expostulations are out of place for the Minister, they are even more so for private persons, unauthorized to challenge the King openly or to "counsel" him publicly.[15]

Donne contrasts not only the manner of petitioning, but also the words. Samuel's words, though authorized, are simply a reminder to God of what God had promised. The Jews' words indicate that they will not trust in God's means or wait for his time to receive their King. Their "clamourous petitions" are a public reproof that Donne contrasts negatively with the forms of prayer authorized for private persons.

Criticizing the King

> That that King that neglects the dutys of his
> place, That exercises his prerogative with out
> iust cause, that vexes his Subiects, nay that giues
> himselfe to intemperate hunting for in that very
> particular, they instance, that in such cases
> kings are as much in theyr mercy, and subiect to

---

[15] This point about authorized means of counsel is discussed in Shami, "Kings."

> censure and correction. we proceed not so in
> censuring the actions of kings. We say with *Ciril*,
> in *John 1.12.56. impium est dicere regi, inique
> agis.*
> (MS Royal, lines 781–90)

> That that King which neglects the duties of his
> place (and they must prescribe the duty, and judge
> the negligence too) That King that exercises his
> Prerogative, without just cause (and they must
> prescribe the Prerogative, and judge the cause,)
> That that King that vexes his Subjects, That that
> King that gives himself to *intemperate hunting*
> (for in that very particular they instance) that
> in such cases, (and they multiply these cases
> infinitely) Kings are in their mercy, and subject
> to their censures, and corrections. We proceed
> not so, in censuring the actions of Kings; we say,
> with St. *Cyrill, Impium est dicere Regi, Inique
> agis; It is an impious thing,* (in him, who is
> onely a private man and hath no other obligations
> upon him) *to say to the King,* or *of the King, He
> governs not as a King is bound to do:*
> (F50, lines 399–408)

Donne specifies more clearly in his revision that his main
objection to the King's critics is that they set themselves up as
lawmakers and judges to the King, appropriating both functions
of prescribing the King's duties and judging the King's negligence.
In the manuscript version, Donne is not denying that the King
is negligent, or that he exercises his prerogative without just
cause. The fault is that the King's critics arrogate to themselves
a public, judicial authority, making themselves the judges of how
the prerogative should be exercised, and in what causes. In addition these critics multiply infinitely the number of cases of the
King's bad behaviour, specifically his "intemperate hunting." In
the revision, Donne explains that this is an impious thing in one
who is only a private person and has no other obligations on him

(as a preacher does) to criticize the King's government. There are judicial avenues for such criticism. Nonetheless, Donne does not free those who are authorized counselors of their responsibility in such matters. For Donne, it is important that people act within authorized political and religious vocations. As with the previous revision on Samuel and the Jews, Donne focuses on the responsibilities of the people to whom he is preaching, rather than on judgment of their substantive, and perhaps legitimate, objections.

Excusing the Prince

> but princes do not so much as worke therein, and
> therefore are excusable.
> (MS Royal, lines 913–14)

> but Princes doe not so much as worke therein, and
> so may bee excusable; at least, for any
> cooperation in the evill of the action, though not
> for countenancing, and authorising an evill
> instrument; but that is another case.
> (F50, lines 477–80)

This addition in 1649 is the most important revision Donne makes. In the manuscript version, Donne appears to be excusing Princes for their part in ill actions, adopting the familiar tactic of blaming officers rather than the source of power. Even God, who permits evil actions, although he does not allow them, could be said to be more implicated than the Prince. But in the revision, Donne does not excuse the Prince for countenancing and authorizing an evil instrument. In fact, he explicitly criticizes such shortsightedness, but ends abruptly without discussing further the nature of the King's responsibility to surround himself with wise counselors. The distinction he makes is an important one; he shifts the focus of responsibility from the agents who execute the Prince's good intentions in a bad way, to the Prince himself who authorized these evil instruments.

Given the crisis of counsel taking place in the 1620s, and particularly the public sense that evil counsel in the person of
Buckingham was responsible for all of the kingdom's ills, the
words added in the revision resonate politically in a way that
qualifies substantially Donne's willingness to work within the
political fiction of "the King can do no wrong."[16] The change
responds, in fact, to the change from the Jacobean world, in
which this fiction was allowed and even encouraged, to the
Caroline world, in which Charles increasingly rejected this form
of criticism. Donne's change responds as much to the realities
of allowable public discourse as it does to Donne's change of
heart or "authorial intentions" on the matter.

The distinction also challenges us to reread Donne's sermons
with a greater awareness of his subtlety of expression. Critics
generally have not responded sensitively to the significance of
Donne's words of qualification in his sermons. They have focused on nouns and verbs, to the exclusion of the adjectives and
adverbs he attached to these. In fact, critics have searched for
easily categorized statements and black-and-white distinctions—
the kind of thing that Donne not only avoids, but that do not
represent the complex and casuistical way in which he handled
moral issues.[17] Because we know a great deal about the circumstances in which these two versions of the Gunpowder Anniversary sermon were produced, we are better able to see the kinds
of changes Donne made when he revised his sermons, and the
kinds of qualifications and discriminations that were important
to him.

---

[16] See Lake (1989) for a discussion of how the idea of a popish conspiracy was a particularly effective variant of the evil-counselor argument by which critics could "excoriate the King's policies and advisers
without directly attacking his person" (92).

[17] The importance of casuistry for Donne is discussed in several
important studies. See Slights, Brown, Shami "Donne's Protestant Casuistry," and Shami "Donne's Sermons" in Works Cited.

Other Rewordings and Revisions

In addition to the substantive revisions we've discussed, some of the most significant rewordings Donne adopts in the source for F50 also focus more sharply on the politics of the sermon. One important theme of the sermon is that even a bad King should be obeyed, although Donne continually stresses that the present situation in England is analogous to that of the good King Josiah rather than of the bad King Zedekiah. Accordingly, Donne alters his earlier source to stress the responsibilities of the King's counselors. Early in the sermon, for example, where the MS had stated that those who have "the great honor, and the great chardge to be near them [Kings]" (lines 146–48) have the duty of "Counsayle," F50 clarifies the point. Donne does not simply want to say that those who are "near" to Kings have the responsibility of counsel, but to stress that he is referring specifically to those who are "near them in that kinde"—that is, those who are officially and legitimately near Kings in the authorized role of counselor (F50, line 74). F50 stresses the responsibilities of these officers of the Court even more intensely that does the MS. In the MS, Donne allows that in a lawful assembly the Elders of Israel could justly open up to Samuel the injustice of his officers; in F50, he focuses this to the "injustice of his greatest Officers" (lines 255–56), suggesting that even the King's favorites could, and should be, legitimately criticized in a lawful forum. F50, however, is less confident than the MS that the King is in the midst of *"Tutelar Angels, Nationall Angels"* (F50, lines 754–55). Rather than simply asserting that this is so, F50 adds parenthetically "as it becomes us to hope."

The changes recorded in F50 also specify more clearly the nature of the King's responsibilities in matters of religion. The manuscript states simply that "his end beeing to aduance gods truth, you are bound to trust him with the way" (lines 1083–85); in F50, the wording is "His end being to advance Gods truth, he is to be trusted much, in matters of *indifferent* nature, by the way" (568–70). This statement emphasizes what Donne has already stressed in both versions of the sermon: though the King is a King of men, both in their bodies and souls, he is so only in circumstantial rather than fundamental matters.

The rewordings embodied in F50 also draw attention to the kind of moderate response appropriate even to genuine abuses of royal power. Several changes stress the contrast between Nero and Josiah. In F50, the contrast is not between a bad and a good ruler, but between two rulers who both began well, though only one continued in this way. Donne's point seems to be that the key is not in a good beginning but in persevering in that goodness. In Donne's view, the Josiah of our times has done just that, not turning aside to the separatists or the Papists (F50, lines 315–21). And following his discussion of how the King's good intentions are corrupted in the execution, Donne adds "The thing was good in the roote, and the ill cannot be removed in an instant" (436–37). The patience invoked here is tied as well to moderation in responding to such abuses. In 1622, Donne said that "whosoeuer hath lamented a danger and then congratulated a deliverance, he will provide against a relapse" (179–82), but in F50 he adds that the provision against relapse applies only to those who lament "in rectified affections," (88–89) rather than in excessive public railing.

Donne also seems to clarify that his primary concern in preaching obedience to the King is political rather than personal. Donne stresses in his revisions the effects on the political stability of the Kingdom of public national obedience, and of the dangers resulting when the King falls in the estimation of other nations. In particular, the revision in F50 exempts outsiders from judgment in this plot (579). More specifically, while the MS says that the peace of the State and the glory of the Gospel depend on sustaining the "outward honor and splendour of the king" (lines 1494–95), F50 adds that these things depend on "the estimation" as well as the outward honour and splendour mentioned in 1622 (776).

Two revisions also alter the sermon's emphasis on the King's religion, a matter which in 1622 was the subject of public concern and which the imposition of the *Directions* had highlighted (Cogswell 32). The manuscript states unequivocally that the King "hath not" left his religion, but this assertion is omitted from F50. The manuscript notes the contrary defamations made against the King by Papists: "Then, that he persecuted theyr religion, when he did not, now that he hath lefte his own religion when he hath not?" (lines 1117–19). F50 omits the last phrase, "when he hath not" (line 588). Similarly, Donne revises to repudiate the assertion that Princes "therefore are" excusable when their good intentions are not well executed (MS Royal, line 914), but that Princes "may be" excusable (F50, line 478). This is a small verbal difference, but the revisions taken together suggest that Donne is expressing himself more precisely and critically in F50 than in the Royal MS.

Near the end of the F50 version, the personal responsibility of auditors is emphasized, no matter what the King does. The manuscript states simply that the doors of the kingdom are the King's, and that they must be left to the King's discretion. Both versions contrast the King's discretion in opening and closing doors with that of auditors who have the responsibility of keeping all right in their homes. But F50 goes further to say "Let him open and shut his dores, as God shall put into his minde" (i.e. with God's guidance), perhaps suggesting that the King needs guidance from God since his counsellors have already been shown to be corrupt in their execution of his good intentions (F50, line 793).

IIMPORTANCE OF THE AUTHORIAL SERMON MANUSCRIPT

The discovery and identification of an authorial sermon manuscript corrected in Donne's hand, then, are important for many reasons. The manuscript documents the text of a sermon written down and transcribed in fair copy within days of its delivery in the pulpit, and reveals much about Donne's processes of composition, proofreading, correction and transmission of sermon texts. Scholars of sermon texts of this period have often been frustrated because the relation between what was said in the pulpit and what was finally published was not known. While we have always assumed that a sermon for publication would differ from the sermon as delivered, we have not previously had such a precise instrument of comparison.

The two states of the sermon as we have them suggest that Donne changed his sermons not only for stylistic or rhetorical reasons, but also for political ones (and probably for many others we cannot determine); however, both versions of the sermon speak for their time and place. This means that the question of determining which text is closest to Donne's intentions, either verbally or politically, is perhaps the wrong question. Many of the revisions indicate that Donne's intentions changed. The circumstances surrounding this sermon, and the nature of Donne's revisions to the manuscript when he prepared it for publication, tell us something of his sense of decorum in the pulpit. A comparison of the two versions reinforces the sense that Donne is concerned with authorized means of criticism, but that in 1622 he was wary of criticizing the King as openly as he did in the revised version. In fact, the crucial passages, politically, reveal both what Donne's views were about the King's responsibility not to countenance bad counselors, and his own sense that November 1622 was not the right time, given the prevailing conditions of censorship that he himself had defended, for making such a criticism.

In conclusion, however wary we are of applying concepts of authority and intention to the textual and historical study of this new Donne manuscript, it seems clear to me that we cannot eliminate them altogether. Nor would that assist us in making sense of the material in front of us. If anything, we need to know more about Donne as author and corrector of his sermon manuscripts, and this discovery at least sets us on the path of an enriched historical understanding of his sermons and their cultural production and transmission.

Works Cited

Alford, Henry, ed. *The Works of John Donne, D.D.* 6 vols. London, 1839.

Allen, D. C. "Dean Donne Sets His Text." *ELH* 10 (1943): 208–29.

Bald, R. C. *John Donne: A Life.* Oxford: Clarendon Press, 1970.

Barker, Nicolas. "Donne's 'Letter to the Lady Carey and Mrs. Essex Riche': Text and Facsimile." *The Book Collector* 22 (1973): 487–93.

Barker, Nicolas. "'Goodfriday 1613': by whose hand?". *Times Literary Supplement*, 20 September 1974: 996–97.

Baugh, Albert C., and Thomas Cable. *A History of the English Language.* 4th ed. Englewood Cliffs, N.J.: Prentice-Hall, 1993.

Beal, Peter. *Index of English Literary Manuscripts. 1450–1625.* Vol. 1. Part 1. London: Mansell, 1980.

British Library. *Class Catalogue of MSS. Theology. Sermons and Treatises (Anglo-Saxon and English).*

Brown, Meg Lota. *John Donne and the Politics of Conscience in Early Modern England.* Leiden: E. J. Brill, 1995.

Burgin, Terry, and John Wall. "'This sermon . . . upon the Gun-powder day': The Book of Homilies of 1547 and Donne's Sermon in Commemoration of Guy Fawkes' Day, 1622." *South Atlantic Review* 49.2 (1984): 19–30.

Casley, David. *A Catalogue of the Manuscripts in the King's Library: An Appendix to the Catalogue of the Cottonian Library.* London, 1734.

Cogswell, Thomas. *The Blessed Revolution: English Politics and the Coming of War, 1621–24.* Cambridge: Cambridge University Press, 1989.

Croft, P. J. *Autograph Poetry in the English language.* Vol. 1: 25–6. New York: McGraw-Hill, 1973.

De Grazia, Margaret, and Peter Stallybrass. "The Materiality of the Shakespearean Text." *Shakespeare Quarterly* 44.3 (1993): 255–83.

Donne, John. *Fifty Sermons*. London, 1649.

———. *Letters to Severall Persons of Honour (1651)*. Ed. M. Thomas Hester. Delmar, N.Y.: Scholars' Facsimiles & Reprints, 1977.

———. *LXXX Sermons*. London, 1640.

Fincham, Kenneth, ed. *Visitation Articles and Injunctions of the Early Stuart Church*. Vol. 1. Church of England Record Society: The Boydell Press, 1994.

Foucault, Michel. "What is An Author?" Trans. Josue V. Harari. *The Foucault Reader*. Ed. Peter Rabinow, 101–120. New York: Pantheon Books, 1984.

Gardner, Helen. *John Donne's Holograph of 'A Letter to the Lady Carey and Mrs Essex Riche'*. Oxford: Scolar Mansell, 1972.

Gray, Dave and Jeanne Shami. "Political Advice in Donne's *Devotions*: No Man is an Island." *Modern Language Quarterly* 50 (1989): 337–56.

Harland, Paul W. "Donne's Political Intervention in the Parliament of 1629." *John Donne Journal* 11.1–2 (1992): 21–37.

Haskin, Dayton. "John Donne and the Cultural Contradictions of Christmas." *John Donne Journal* 11.1–2 (1992): 133–57.

Heawood, Edward. *Watermarks: Mainly of the 17th and 18th Centuries*. Hilversum: Paper Publications Society, 1950.

Hill, W. Speed. "Editing Nondramatic Texts of the English Renaissance: A Field Guide with Illustrations." *New Ways of Looking at Old Texts*. Ed. W. Speed Hill. 1–24. Binghamton, N.Y.: Medieval & Renaissance Texts & Studies, 1993.

———. "The Calculus of Error, or Confessions of a General Editor." *Modern Philology* 76 (1978): 247–60.

Lake, Peter. "Anti-popery: The Structure of a Prejudice." *Conflict in Early Stuart England*. Eds. Richard Cust and Ann Hughes, 72–106. London: Longman, 1989.

McGann, Jerome. *A Critique of Modern Textual Criticism*. Chicago: University of Chicago Press, 1983.

————. "The Monks and the Giants: Textual and Bibliographical Studies and the Interpretation of Literary Works." *Textual Criticism and Literary Interpretation.* Ed. Jerome McGann, 180–99. Chicago: University of Chicago Press, 1985.

Norbrook, David. "The Monarchy of Wit and the Republic of Letters: Donne's Politics." *Soliciting Interpretation: Literary Theory and Seventeenth-Century English Poetry.* Eds. Elizabeth Harvey and Katherine Maus, 3–36. Chicago: University of Chicago Press, 1990.

Patterson, Annabel. "All Donne." *Soliciting Interpretation: Literary Theory and Seventeenth-Century English Poetry.* Eds. Elizabeth Harvey and Katherine Maus, 37–67. Chicago: University of Chicago Press, 1990.

————. "John Donne, Kingsman?" *The Mental World of the Jacobean Court.* Ed. Linda Levy Peck, 251–72. Cambridge: Cambridge University Press, 1991.

————. "Misinterpretable Donne: The Testimony of the Letters." *John Donne Journal* 1 (1982): 39–53.

Pebworth, Ted-Larry, and Ernest W. Sullivan, II. "Rational Presentation of Multiple Text Traditions." *Papers of the Bibliographical Association of America* 83 (1989): 43–60.

Pebworth, Ted-Larry. "Manuscript Transmission and the Selection of Copy-Text in Renaissance Coterie Poetry." *TEXT* 7 (1995): 243–61.

Petti, Anthony G. *English Literary Hands from Chaucer to Dryden,* 96–97. London, E. Arnold, 1977.

Potter, George, and Evelyn Simpson, eds. *The Sermons of John Donne.* 10 vols. Berkeley: University of California Press, 1953–62.

Shami, Jeanne. "Donne's Sermons and The Absolutist Politics of Quotation." *Donne's Religious Imagination: Essays in Honor of John T. Shawcross.* Eds. Frances Malpezzi and Raymond-Jean Frontain, 380–412. Conway, AK: University of Central Arkansas Press, 1995.

————. "Donne's 1622 Sermon on the Gunpowder Plot: His Original Presentation Manuscript Discovered." *English Manuscript Studies* 5 (1994): 63–86.

————. "Introduction: Reading Donne's Sermons." *John Donne Journal* 11.1–2 (1992): 1–20.

————. "Kings and Desperate Men: John Donne Preaches at Court." *John Donne Journal* 6.1 (1987): 9–23.

Shillingsburg, Peter L. *Scholarly Editing in the Computer Age: Theory and Practice.* Athens, Ga.: University of Georgia Press, 1986.

Slights, Camille Wells. *The Casuistical Tradition in Shakespeare, Donne, Herbert, and Milton.* Princeton: Princeton University Press, 1972.

Sullivan, Ernest W., ed. *Biathanatos.* Newark: University of Delaware Press, 1984.

Warner, Sir George F., and Julius P. Gilson. *Catalogue of Western Manuscripts in the Old Royal and King's Collections.* Vol. 2. London: Longman, Green & Co., 1921.

Werstine, Paul. "Narratives About Printed Shakespearean Texts: 'Foul Papers' and 'Bad' Quartos." *Shakespeare Quarterly* 41.1 (1990): 65–86.

————. "The Textual Mystery of *Hamlet.*" *Shakespeare Quarterly* 39.1 (1988): 1–26.

Wolff, Janet. *The Social Production of Art.* 1981. New York: New York University Press, 1984.

Zeller, Hans. "A New Approach to the Critical Constitution of Literary Texts." *Studies in Bibliography* 28 (1975): 231–64.

John Donne's 1622
Gunpowder Plot Sermon

Facsimile & Transcription

Notes on Transcription

This transcription is a diplomatic rendering of the manuscript, in keeping with the modern documentary intention of this edition. Modern italic type is used to represent scribal italics. Secretary hand is printed as roman type. Boldface is used to indicate Donne's corrections as well as corrections possibly by Donne. Passages underlined are to be compared with substantive variants from F50 at the bottom of the page. All variants from F50 are included here except the "Prayer Before the Sermon," which is not present in the manuscript copy but appears in 1649 with the first printed version of the sermon.

Short forms have not been expanded; *i* and *j*, *u* and *v* have not been normalized, although the long *s* has been. I have also normalized *ff* to *F*. I have transcribed the symbol for *es* (*ʃ*) as *s*. This decision is based on my judgment that the scribe does not distinguish consistently between the two forms of final *s*, and that the *es* transcription would create confusing spellings [i.e., *ies* for *is*]. I have transcribed the symbol for *per* as *p[er]* (it occurs only once in the manuscript). Majescule *L* is difficult to identify in this manuscript, since what might be taken for this letter often appears medially or at the beginning of a portion of a hyphenated word. I have chosen to represent *l's* as miniscule on the grounds that capitalization is slight in this manuscript; many words that would normally be capitalized according to modern conventions are not capitalized in this manuscript (i.e. the word *god* or words following a full stop).

An asterisk in the margin indicates that there is a note on the transcription in Appendix B.

17.13 XX . p. 264.

Lamentati: 4. 20. The breath of our Nostrills
the Anointed of the Lord was taken in
their pitts.

Of the Autor of this booke, I thinke there
was never doubt made. but yet it is scarse
safely done by the Councell of Trent, when
in that Canon wth numbers the bookes of
Canonicall Scriptures they leave out
this booke of Lamentations. for, though
I make no doubt but that they had a
purpose to comprehend and involue yt in
the name of Ieremy, yet that was not in=
ough; for so they might haue comprehen=
ded and involue Genesis and Deuterono=
mie and all between, in one name of Moses:
and so they might haue comprehended
and involue, the Apocalypse and ~~John~~ some
Epistles in the name of Iohn, and haue
left out this booke it selfe in the number.
But one of their ~~owne~~ Iesuits, though some

*Lame**ntati**: 4. 20. The breath of our Nostrills,*
  the Anointed of the Lord was taken in
  their pitts.

Of the Autor of this booke I thinke there   1

was never doubt made. but yet <u>it</u> is scarse   2

safely donne <u>by the Councell of Trent, when</u>   3

*   in that Cannon wch numbers the books of   4

Canonicall Scriptures <u>they</u> leave out   5

this booke of lamentations. for, though   6

I make no doubt but that they had a   7

purpose to comprehend and inuolue yt in   8

the name of *Jeremy*, yet that was not in=   9

ough; for so they might haue comprehen=   10

ded and inuolud *Genesis* and *Deuterono=*   11

mie and all <u>between</u>, in one name of *Moses*:   12

and so they might haue comprehended   13

*   and inuolud, the *Apocalypse* and ~~Johns~~ **some**   14

Epistles ~~as~~ **in** the name of *John*, and haue   15

left out the booke it selfe in the number.   16

But one of their owne Iesuits, though   17
                                              some

---

2   that
3   which the *Councell of Trent* doth,
5   to
12   between those two

some, (whome in that Canon they seeme to
Castro: haue follow'd) make this booke of Lamen=
tations but an Appendix to the booke of
Jeremie, determins for all that Canon,
that it is a distinct booke; Indeed, if it
were not, the first Chapter would haue
been call'd the 53.th of Jeremy. and not the
first of the Lamentations. But that
wth giues most assurednes to it, is, that in
diuers Heb: Bibles it is plac'd other=
wise, then we place it; not presently)
after the prophecy of Jeremy though
it were euer undoubtedly receyued to be
his.

The booke is certainly the prophet Je=
remies: and certainly a distinct booke,
but whether the booke be a History, or
a prophecy, whether Jer: lament'd,
wch he had seene, or that wch he
foresees, calamities past, or future
                                   calamities.

some, (whome in that Canon they seeme to | 18

Castro. haue followd,) make this booke of *lamen=* | 19

tations but an Appendix to the booke of | 20

Jeremie, determins for all that Canon, | 21

that it is a distinct booke; Indeed, if it | 22

were not, the first Chapter would haue | 23

been calld the 53th of *Jeremy*: and not the | 24

* first of the *Lamentations*. But that | 25

wch giues most assurednes to it, is, that in | 26

divers *Heb:* Bibles it is placd other= | 27

wise, then we place it; not presently | 28

after the prophecy, of *Jeremy* though | 29

it were ever vndoubtedly receyud to be | 30

his. | 31

The booke is certainly the prophet *Je=* | 32

remies: and certainly a distinct booke; | 33

but whether the booke be a history, or | 34

a prophecy, whether *Jer:* lament y^t, | 35

which he had seene, or that which he | 36

foresees, calamities past, or future | 37
calamities

---

19   follow
20   Prophecy
24   53
26   assurednesse
28   and not presently, and immediately
29–30   but discontinued from him, though hee were never doubted
31   the Author thereof

calamities, thinges donne, or thinges to be
donne, is a question which hath exercised
and busied diuers expositors. But as
we say of the parable of <u>Diues</u> and
<u>Lazarus</u>, that it is an historicall pa-
rable, and a parabolicall history, some
such persons there were, and some such
thinges were really donne, but some
other thinges were figuratiuely, Symbolically, parabolically added, So we say
of <u>Ieremies Lamentations</u>, it is a
propheticall history, and it is a histori-
rall prophesy; some of these sad occasions of these Lamentations were past,
when he writt, and some were to come
after: for we may not despise the testimo-
nie of the Chalde paraphrase who were
the first that illustrated the Bible in
that nation, nor of S^t: Hiero: who was
much conuersant with the Bible, and
                                    with

calamities, things donne, or things to be 38

donne, is a question which hath exercisd 39

and busied divers expositors. But as 40

we say of the parable of *Diues* and 41

* *Lazarus*, that it is <u>an</u> historicall pa= 42

rable, and a parabolicall history, some 43

such persons there were, and some such 44

things were really donne, but some 45

other things were figuratively, Sym= 46

bolically, parabolically added, So we say 47

of *Jeremies lamentations*, it is a 48

propheticall history, <u>and it is a</u> histori= 49

call prophecy; some of <u>these</u> sad occasi= 50

ons of these lamentations were past, 51

when he writt, and some were to come 52

after: for we may not despise the testimo= 53

nie of the Chalde paraphrasts who were 54

the first that illustrated the Bible in 55

that Nation, nor of *Se: Hiero*: who was 56

much conuersant with the Bible, and 57
       with

---

42 a
48 *Lamentation*
49 and a
50 the

with that Nation, now of Josephus who had
justly so much estimation in that Nation, now of
those later Rabbins who were ye learnedest of ye Nation,
who are all of opinion, that Jer: writt
these Lamentations after he sawe some
declinations in that state in the death of
Josiah, and so the booke is Historicall, but
when he onely foresaw, their transportation
into Babilon, and before yt fell vppon them,
and so it is propheticall. Or if we take
the exposition of the others, That the whole
booke was written after their transportation into Babylon, and so be in all,
Historicall, yet it is propheticall still,
for the prophet laments a greater de=
solation then yt, in the vtter ruine
and devastation of that Citty and Nation
after the death of Christ Jesus: Neyther
is any peece of this booke, the lesse fitt
to be our text, this day, because it is
both Historicall and propheticall; for,
they from whome god in his great
mercy, gaue vs a deliverance this day
are

with that Nation, nor of *Josephus* who had   58

iustly so much estimation in that Nation, nor of   59

those later Rabbins who were ye learnedest of y^t Nation,   60

who are all of opinion, that *Jer:* writt   61

these lamentations after he sawe some   62

declinations in that state in the death of   63

Josiah, and so the booke is Historicall, but   64

when he onely foresaw, their transportation   65

into *Babilon*, <u>and before y^t</u> fell vpon them,   66

and so it is propheticall. Or if we take   67

the exposition of the others, That the whole   68

booke was written after their transpor=   69

tation into *Babylon*, and <u>so be in all</u>,   70

historicall, yet it is propheticall still;   71

for the prophet laments a greater de=   72

solation <u>them</u> y^t, in the vtter ruine   73

and devastation of <u>that</u> Citty and Nation   74

<u>after</u> the death of Christ Iesus: Neyther   75

is any peece of this booke, the lesse fitt   76

to be our text, this day, because it is   77

both Historicall and propheticall; for,   78

they from whome god in <u>his great</u>   79

<u>mercy,</u> gaue vs a deliverance this day,   80

are

66	before that calamity
70	to be, in all parts
73	then
74	the
75	which was to fall upon them, after
79–80	his mercy

our historicall enemies, and our prophe=
ticall enemies; historically we know, they
haue attempted our ruine heretofore,
and prophetically we may be sure, they
will do so againe, when soeuer any new
occasion prouokes them, or sufficient
power enables them.

The text then is as the booke presented to
Ezechiel. in it are written Lamentations,
and mournings, and wo: and all they are
written within, and without, says the text
there: within, as they concerne the Iews,
without as they are appliable to vs. And
they concerne the Iews, historically, At=
tempts vpon that state, Ieremie had cer=
taynely shewe, and they concerne them pro=
phetically, farther attempts Ieremie
did certainely foresee. They are appli=
able to vs so to; historically, we saw
what they would haue donne; propheti=
cally, we foresee what they would do.

so

<u>our</u> Historicall enemies, and our prophe=   81

ticall enemies; historically we know, they   82

haue attempted our ruine heretofore,   83

and prophetically we may be sure, they   84

*   will do so againe; when soever any new   85

occasion provokes them, or sufficient   86

power enables them.   87

The text then is as the booke presented to   *Diuisio*   88

Ezechiel. in it are written lamentations,   *2.20.*   89

*   and <u>mourninge</u>, and wo: and all they are   90

written within, and with out, says the Text   91

there: within, as they concerne the Iews,   92

without as they are appliable to vs. And   93

they concerne the Iews, historically, At=   94

tempts vpon that state, *Jeremie* had cer=   95

taynely seene, and they concerne them pro=   96

phetically, <u>farther</u> attempts *Jeremie*   97

did certainely foresee. They are appli=   98

able to vs <u>so to; historically; we saw</u>   99

what they would haue donne; <u>propheti=</u>   100

<u>cally,</u> we foresee what they would do.   101
so

---

81   are our
88–89M   Divisio./Ezek.2.20.
90   *Mournings*
97   for farther
99   both ways too: *Historically*, because wee have seen
100–01   And *Prophetically*, because

So that here is but a difference of the
Computation; here is Stilo veteri and
Stilo novo: here the Jews Calender
and the Papists Calender. In the Jews
Calender one Babilon wrought upon the
people of god, and in the Papists Calender, an other Babilon; Stilo veteri in
the Jews Calender 700 year before
Christ came, there were pitts made,
and the breath of our Nostrills, the A-
nointed of the Lord was taken in their
pitts. Stilo novo in the Papists Ca=
lender, 1600 year after Christ came
in all fullnes in all clearnes, there
were pitts made againe, and the breath
of our Nostrills, the Anointed of the
Lord was taken in their pitts.
At is Jeremies, and a distinct booke; it
concernes the Jews, and vs too; and
both, both ways; but whether Jeremie
lament here the death of a good king
                         Josias

So that here is but a difference of the 102

Computation; here is *Stilo veteri*, and 103

Stilo nouo: <u>her's</u> the Iews Calender 104

and the Papists Cᵃlender. In the Iews 105

Calender one *Babilon* wrought vpon the 106

people of god, and in the Papists Calen= 107

* der, an other *Babilon*; *Stilo veteri* in 108

the Iews Calender 700 year before 109

Christ came, There were pitts made, 110

* and *the breath of <u>our</u> Nostrills, the An=* 111

nointed of the lord was taken in their 112

pitts. Stilo nouo in the Papists Ca= 113

lender, 1600 year after Christ came 114

in all fullnes, in all clearnes, There 115

were pitts made againe, and *the breath* 116

* *of our Nostrills, the Annointed of the* 117

lord was <u>taken in their</u> pitts. 118

It <u>is *Ieremies*; and</u> a distinct booke; it 119

concernes the Iews, <u>and</u> vs too; and 120

<u>both, both ways</u>; but whether *Ieremie* 121

lament here the death of a good King 122
                                Iosias

104 here is
111 *their*
118 *almost taken in those*
119 is then *Ieremies*, and it is
120 and it concerns
121 it concernes us both, *both wayes, Historically*, and *Prophetically*

Josias, (for so S: Hierome and many of
the ancients, and many of the Iews
themselfs take it, and hence that these
words have relation to these lamentations, And Ieremie lamented for Iosiah,
and all the people speake of him in
their lamentations to this day), and
behold they are written in their lamentations) or whether he lament the transportation and the misery of an yll
kñg of Zedichia, (as is more ordina-
rilie and more probably sett by the
expositors,) we argue not we dispute
not now: we embrace that which ari-
ses from both, that both good kñg,
and bad kñg Iosiah and Zedichia,
are the anointed of the Lord, and the
breath of the Nostrills, that is, the
lyfe of their people; and therefore
both to be lamented when they fall
into dangers, and consequently both
to be

2 par:
35.25.

Iosias, (for so _S: Hierome_ and many of 123

the ancients, and many of the Iews 124

themselfs take it, and thinke that those 125

words haue relation to these lamenta= 126

2 par:

tions, And _Jeremie_ lamented for _Josiah,_ 127

_35.25._

and all the people speake of him in 128

their lamentations to this day, and 129

behold they are written in their lamen= 130

tations) or whether he lament the trans= 131

portation and the misery of an yll 132

King of _Zedichia,_ (as is more ordina= 133

rilie and more probably held by the 134

expositors,) we argue not, we dispute 135

not now: we embrace that which ari= 136

ses from both, that both good Kings, 137

and bad Kings _Josiah_ and _Zedichia,_ 138

are the anointed of the lord, and the 139

breath of the Nostrills, that is, the 140

lyfe of their people; and therefore 141

both to be lamented when they fall 142

into dangers, and consequently both 143
to be

---

123   of _Josiah_
126   words in the _Chronicles_
126–7M 2.35.25.
129–31 _Lamentations,)_
136   now
141   the

to be preserved by all meanes, by prayer
from them who are private persons, by
counsayle from them who have the
great honour, and the great charge
to be near them, and by support and
supplie from all of all sorts, from fal=
linge into sure dangers.

These considerations, will (I thinke) haue
the better impression in you, if we
proceed in the handling of them, thus.

First, the maine cause of the lamentation
was the ruine or the dangerous de=
clination of the kingdome, of that
great and glorious state, the King=
dome. But then they did not sediti=
ously sever the King and the King=
dome, as though the kingdome could
be well, and the King yll; that
safe, and he in danger; they saw
cause to lament, because misery
was fallen vpon the King; yt came
vpon Josiah, a good, a religious
King

to be preservd by all meanes, by prayer   144

from them who are private persons, by   145

Counsayle from them, who haue <u>the</u>   146

great honor, and <u>the</u> great chardge   147

to be <u>near them</u>, and by support and   148

supplie from all of all sorts, from fal=   149

linge into such dangers.   150

These considerations, will, I thinke, haue   151

the better impression in you, if we   152

proceed in the handling of them, thus.   153

First, the maine cause of the lamentation,   154

was the ruine, or the dangerous de=   155

clination of the Kingdome, of that   156

great and glorious state, The King=   157

dome. But then they did not sediti=   158

ously sever the King and the King=   159

dome, as though the Kingdome could   160

<u>be</u> well, and the King yll; that   161

safe, and he in danger; <u>they</u> see   162

cause to lament, because misery   163

was fallen vpon <u>the King</u>; p[er]chance   164

vpon *Josiah,* a good, a religious   165
Kinge

---

146 that
147 that
148 near them in that kinde
161 doe
162 for they
164 *the Person* of *the King*

Kings vppon Iehoaaz: [but] vppon Zedichia a worse
Kinge: yet whichsoever it be, they acknow=
ledge him to be Vnctus ~~Dei~~ Domini,
the anointed of the Lord, and to be Spi=
ritus narium the breath of their Nostrills.
when their person therefore was fall'n
into the pitts of the Enemie, the Sub=
iect laments; but their lamenting,
which was because he was falln, im=
plyes a deliverance, a restitution; he
was falln, but he did not ly there; so
the text which is yet a lamentation,
growes an happie henre to be a congra=
tulation; and then we shall see, that who=
soever hath lamented a danger and then
congratulated a deliverance, he will pro=
vide against a relapse, a falling againe
into that or any other danger, by all
meanes of sustayning the Kingdome,
and the King, in safety, and in honor.
Our first step in their Royall progresse   Regnum
is, that the cause of their lamentation
was,

but
*   Kinge, perchance vpon *Zedichia* a worse   166
             ^

Kinge: yet, which soever it be, they acknow=   167

ledge him to be *Vnctus* D̶ m̶ *Domini,*   168

the anointed of the lord, and to be *Spi=*   169

*   *ritus narium* the breath of their Nostrills.   170

when this person therefore was fall'n   171

into the pitts of the Enemie, the Sub=   172

iect laments; but this lamentinge,   173

<u>which was because</u> he was falln, im=   174

plyes a deliverance, a restitution; he   175

was falln, but he did not ly there; so   176

the text which is <u>yit a</u> lamentation,   177

<u>growes</u> an howre hence to be <u>a</u> congra=   178

tulation; and then we shall see, that <u>who=</u>   179

<u>soeuer</u> hath lamented a danger and then   180

congratulated a deliverance, he will pro=   181

vide against a relapse, a fallinge againe   182

into that or any other danger, by all   183

*   meanes of sustayning the~~at~~ Kingdome,   184

*   and the~~at~~ King, in safety, and in honor.   185

Our first <u>step</u> in this Royall progresse   *1*   186
                                Regnum

is, that the cause of this lamentation   187
             was,

---

174   because
177   as yet but of
178   will grow . . . of
179–80   whosoever, in rectified affections,
186   step then

was the declination, the diminution of the
kingdome. As the Center of the world
could be moved, but one inch, out of the
place, it cannot be reckoned how many
miles this Iland, or any buildings in it,
would be throwen out of their places: A
declination in the kingdome of the soul,
in the body of the kingdome, in the
Soule of that state, that forme of gover=
ment, was such an earthquake, as would
leave nothing standing. Of all things that
are, there was an Idea in god; there
was a Model, a platforme, an exemplar,
of every thing, which god produced, and
created in tyme, in the Minde and pur=
pose of god before. Of all things god
had an Idea, a conception; but of Mo=
narchy, of kingdome, god, who is but
one, is the Idea; god himselfe, in his
unity, is the Model, he is the Type of
Monarchy. He made but one world; this
and the next, are not two worlds; this
is

was the Declination, the diminution of the | 188

Kingdome. If the Center of the world | 189

should be moud, but one inche, out of the | 190

place, it cannot be reckconed how many | 191

miles this Iland, or any <u>buildings</u> in it, | 192

* would be thrown out of their places: A | 193

declination in the kingdome of the Iews, | 194

in the body of the kingdome, in the | 195

Soule of <u>that state, That</u> forme of gouer= | 196

ment, was such an Earthquake, as could | 197

leaue
* ~~leaue~~ nothing standinge. Of all things that | 198
  ^

* are, there was an Idæa in god; there | 199

was a Model, a platforme, an <u>exemplar,</u> | 200

of euery thing, which god producd, and | 201

* created in tyme, in the Minds and pur= | 202

pose of god before. Of all things god | 203

* had an Idæa, a <u>conception</u>; but of Mo= | 204

narchy, of Kingdome, god, who is but | 205

* one, is the Idæa; God himselfe, in his | 206

vnity, is the Model, he is the Type of | 207

Monarchy. He made but one world; <u>this</u> | 208

and the next, are not two worlds; this | 209
                          is

---

192 building
196 the State, in the
200 examplar
204 preconception
208 for, this

6

is but the morninge, and that the ever=
lasting Noone, of one and the same day,
which shall have no night. they are not
two houses; Tis the gallery, that the bec=
chamber of one and the same pallace
which shall feele no ruine. He made this
one world, but one Eye, the Sun; the
Moone is not another Ey, but a glasse
vpon which the Sun reflects. He made
this one world but one Eare, the Church:
he tells not vs that he heard in a loft eare,
by faith. but by this right eare, the Church,
he does. One god, one faith, one Baptisme,
and these leade vs to the end of one Souer=
aigne, of Monarchy, of kingdome. In that
name he hath conuayd to vs the state of
grace, and the state of Glorie too; and
promisd both, in enioyninge that prayer
Adueniat regnum; the kingdome of
grace here, the kingdome of Glorie
hereafter. All formes of gouerment
haue the same Soule, Soueraintey; that
resides somewhere, in every forme; and
      this

is but the morninge, and that the ever=   210

lasting Noone, of one and the same day,   211

which shall haue no night. they are not   212

two howses; <u>This the</u> gallery, <u>that</u> the bed=   213

chamber of one and the same pallace   214

which shall feele no ruine. He made this   215

one world, but one Eye, The Sun; the   216

Moone is not another Ey, but a glasse   217

vpon which the Sun reflects. He made   218

this one world but one Ear, The Church: 219

he tells not vs that he hears <u>in</u> a left ear,   220

by Saints. but by <u>his</u> right ear, the Church,   221

he <u>does. One</u> god, one faith, one Baptisme,   222

and these leade vs to the loue of one Souer=   223

aigne, of Monarchy, of Kingdome. In that   224

name <u>he</u> hath convayd to vs the state of   225

grace, and the state of Glorie too; and   226

<u>promisd</u> both, in enioyninge that <u>prayer,</u>   227

<u>*Adueniat regnum*</u>; Thy kingdome of   228

grace here, thy kingdome of Glorie   229

hereafter. All formes of goverment   230

haue <u>the same</u> Soule, <u>Souerainty</u>; that   231

resides some where, in euery forme; and   232
                                             this

---

213   This is the . . . and that
220   by
221   that
222   doth. There is *One*
225   God
227   he hath promised . . . Petition
228   *Adveniat Regnum, Thy Kingdome come*
231   one and the same . . . that is, *Soveraignty*

this Soueraulty is from the same roote in them all; from the Lord of Lords, from God himselfe, for all power is of God: but yet this forme of a Monarchy, of a kingdome, is a more liuely, and a more masculin organ, and instrument of this Soule of Soueraynty, then the other formes are. We are sure women haue Souls as well as Men; but yet it is not expressed, that God breathed a Soule into woman as he did into Man: All formes of gouernment haue this Soule, but yet god infused it more manifestly, and more effectually in that forme, in a kingdome. All places are a= like near to heauen; yet the will would take a hill for the place of his Ascension. All gouernments may rightly represent god to me, who is the god of order, and foun= taine of all gouernment. But yet I am more cast and more accustomd to the con= templation of heauen in that notion, as a kingdome, by hauing been borne and bread in a Monarchy. God is a type of it, and yet is a type of heauen.

this

this Souerainty is <u>from the same roote in</u>

233

<u>them all</u>; from the lord of lords, from god

234

himselfe, for all power is of god: but yet

235

this forme of a Monarchy, of a kingdome,

236

is a more liuely, and a more masculin

237

organ, and instrument of this Soule of

238

Souerainty, then the other formes are.

239

We are sure women haue Souls as well

240

as Men; but yet it is <u>not expressd</u>, that

241

god breathd a Soule into woman as he

242

did into Man: All formes of goverment

243

haue this Soule, but yet god <u>infuses</u> it more

244

manifestly, and more effectually in that

245

forme, in a kingdome. All places are a=

246

like near to heaven; yet Christ would take

247

a hill <u>for the place of</u> his Ascension. All

248

goverments may iustly represent god to

249

me, who is the god of Order, and foun=

250

taine of all gouerment. But yet I am

251

more easd and more accustomd to the con=

252

templation of heauen in that notion, <u>as</u>

253

<u>a</u> kingdome, by hauing been borne and

254

bread in a Monarchy. God is a Tipe of

255

<u>it; and yt</u> ys a tipe of heauen.

256

this

233–34 in them all, from one and the same *Root*
241   not so expressed
244   infuseth
248   for
252–3   as *Heaven is a*
256   that, and that

This forme then, in nature the noblest, and in
is the profitablest of all other, God allwayes
intended to give his best beloued people; God
allwayes ment that the Iewes should haue a king,
though he prepard them in other formes be=
fore; he ment them peace at last, though
he exercisd them in war; he ment them
the land of promise, though he led them
through the wildernes; he ment them a
king though he prepard them by Iudges.
God intended it in himselfe, and he declard
it to them: 400 yeares before he gaue them
a king, he told them what kind of king
they should sett ouer them, when they came
to that kind of gouernment. And longe be=
fore that he made a promise by Iacob to
Iudah of a kingdome, and that the Scep=
ter should not depart from him till Si=
loh came. And when god came near the
tyme, in which he intended them that
gouernment, in the tyme of Samuel,
who was his immediat ~~~~~ predecessor
to their

Judaeis
promissa.

Deu:17:
14.

Gen:49.
10.

his forme then, in nature the noblest, <u>and in</u>   *Judæis*   257
                                                          promissa.

vse the profitablest of all <u>other</u>, God allways   258

intended to his best beloued people; God   259

* allways ment that the Iews should haue a king,   260

though he prepard them in other formes be=   261

fore; <u>he</u> ment them peace at last, though   262

he exercisd them in war; <u>he</u> ment them   263

the land of promise, though he led them   264

through the wildernes; <u>he</u> ment them a   265

King though he prepard them by Iudges.   266

God intended it in himselfe, and he declard   267

it to them: 400 years before he <u>gaue</u> them   *Deu:17:*   268
                                                                14.

a king, he <u>told</u> them what kind of King   269

they should sett ouer them, when they came   270

* to that kinde of gouerment. And longe be=   271

fore that, he made a promise by *Jacob* to   *Gen: 49.*   272
                                                            10.

Judah of a kingdome, and that the Scep=   273

ter should not depart from him till *Si=*   274

loh came. And when god came near the   275

tyme, in which he intended <u>them</u> that   276

gouerment, in the tyme of *Samuel,*   277

* who was the immediat --------- predecessor   278
                                    to their

---

257   in
258   others
262   As hee
263   and
265   so he
268   have
269   instructed
276   to them

to their first king Saul, God made way
for a Monarchy; for Samuel had a much
more absolute autority in that state, then
any of the Iudges had; Samuel iudged
them; and in their petition for a king
1 Sam: 8.5.   they aske but that, Make vs a king to
iudge vs. Samuel was litle lesse then
a king: and Sauls raigne and his are
reckned in one number and made alone.
When that is said that Saul reignd 40
Act: 13.21.   yeares, Samuels tyme is included; for
all the yeares from the death of Heli, to
the begining of Dauid are but 40.
God ment them a kingdome in Exodus,
promisd them a kingdome in Iudah,
made lawes for the kingdome in Deute=
ronomie, made way for the kingdome
in Samuel; and why then was God
displeasd with their petition for a king?

It was a greater fault in them, then it
could haue bene in any other people, to
aske a king: not that that was not the
most

	to their first King *Saul,* God made way	279
	for a Monarchy; for *Samuel* had a much	280
	more absolute autority in that state, then	281
*	any of the Iudges had; *Samuel* iudged	282
	them; and in their petition for a king	283
1 Sam: 8:5.	they aske but that, Make vs a king to	284
	iudge vs. *Samuel* was litle lesse then	285
*	a king: and *Sauls* raigne and his are	286
	reckned <u>in</u> one number and made <u>all one.</u>	287
Act: 13.21.	<u>when that is said</u> that *Saul* reignd 40	288
	years, *Samuels* tyme is <u>included</u>; for	289
	all the years, from the death of <u>*Heli,*</u> to	290
	the begining of *Dauid* are but <u>40</u>.	291
	God ment them a kingdome in himselfe,	292
	promisd them a kingdome ^{to} in *Judah,*	293
	made laws for <u>the</u> kingdome in *Deute=*	294
	ronomie, made way for the kingdome	294
	in *Samuel*; and why then was god	296
	displeasd with their petition for a <u>king</u>?	297
	<s>It</s> It was a greater fault in them, then it	298
	could haue bene in any other people, to	299
	aske a king: not that <u>that</u> was not the	300

most

287 both in . . . as the reign of one man
288 when it is said in the *Acts*
289 included in that number
290 *Eli*
291 40 years
294 their
297 Kingdome
300 it

most desirable forme of gouernment, but
that he gouernd them so immediatly, so
presentially himselfe, as that it was an
ingratefull intemperance in them to turne
vpon any other meanes. God had euen
performed that which he promissd; ye
shall be a peculiar treasure vnto me
aboue all people; And therefore Iosephus hath
expressd it well, All other people are
vnder the forme of democratie or Arist-
or shure,
terratie composd of men, — Sed noster .
legislator theocratiam instituit he doub..
were onely vnder a theocratie, an immediat gouernment of god; he iudged
them himselfe, and he fought their
battayls himselfe, and therefore he
sayd to Samuel, they haue not reiected thee, thou wast not king, but they
I was.
gaue reiected me, to be weary of god,
ys it inough, to call it a leuity? But if
they did onely compare forme with forme,
and not god himselfe with any forme
if they did onely thinke a Monarchy both,
and,

Exo: 19.
5.

most desirable forme of gouerment, but 301

that <u>he</u> governd them so immediatly, so 302

presentially himselfe, as that it was an 303

ingratefull intemperance in them to turne 304

vpon any other meanes. God had ever 305

performd that which he <u>promisd</u>; ye 306

shall be a peculiar treasure vnto me 307
  all
aboue people; And therefore *Josephus* hath   *Exo: 19.* 308
  ^   *5.*

expressd it well; All other people are 309

vnder the forme of Democratie or Aris= 310
  or such,
* tocratie composd of Men, ~~or~~ *Sed noster* 311
   ^

legislator theocratiam instituit:. The Iews 312

were onely vnder a Theocratie, an im= 313

mediat goverment of god; he iudged 314

them himselfe, and <u>he fought their</u> 315

<u>battayls himselfe.</u> and therefore <u>he</u> 316

says to *Samuel,* They haue not reiec= 317

ted thee, Thou wast not king, but they 318
   I was.
* haue reiected me; To be weary of god, 319
     ^

ys it inough to call it a leuity? But if 320

they did onely compare forme with forme, 321

and not god himselfe with any forme, 322

if they did onely thinke <u>a Monarchy</u> best, 323
          and

---

302 God
306 promised them, in that which comprehended all
311 or such other formes
315–16 hee himselfe fought their battels
316 God
323 Monarchy

and beleeve that god intended a Monarchy
to them, yet to limit god his tymes, and to
make god performe his promise before
his day, was a fault inexcusable. Daniel sawe that the Messias should come within
70 weekes; Daniel did not say, Lord let
it be within 60 weekes, or let it be this-
weeke. The Martyrs under the Altar,
they cry vsq; quo Domine. but yet they
leave it there; even as long as yt pleaseth
thee. There petition should have beene
Adueniat regnum, lett have that kingz
dome, weire, because thou knowest it is
good for vs, thou hast promised to vs,
but yet fiat voluntas tua, lett-
have it then, when thy wisdome sees it
best for vs. you said to me sayth Samuel, 1 Samuel 12-12-Nay, but a king
shall raigne over vs, when the Lord
your god was your king. They would
not trust gods meanes, there was their
first fault; And then George they desird
a good king, and intended to them, yet
they)

and beleeve that god intended a Monarchy 324

to them, yet to limit god his <u>tymes</u>, and to 325

make god perfor_e^m his promise before 326

  * his day, was a fault <u>in excusable</u>. *Dani=* 327

el saw that the Messias should come within 328

70 weekes; *Daniel* did not say, lord let 329

it be within 50 weeks, or let it be this 330

weeke. The Martyrs vnder the Altar, 331

  * they cry *vsq[ue] quo Domine.* <u>but yet</u> they 332

leaue it there; euen as long as <u>yt please</u> 333

  ~ thee. <u>There</u> petition should haue beene, 334

Adueniat regnum, <u>lets</u> haue that king= 335

dome, which, because thou knowest it is 336

good for vs, thou hast promisd to vs, 337

but yet *fiat voluntas tua,* <u>lets</u> 338

haue it then, when thy wisedome sees it 339

best for vs. you said to me, says *Sa=* 340

  * muel, <u>*1 Samuel 12.12.*</u> Nay but a king 341

shall ræigne <u>over vs</u>, when the lord 342

your god, was your king. They would 343

  * not trust gods meanes, the~~i~~re was their 344

  * first fault; And then though they desird 345

<u>a good thing, and intended to them</u>, yet 346
                                   they

325 *time*
327 and inexcusable
332 cry *Vsquequo Domine, How long Lord,* but then,
333 pleaseth
334 Their
335 *Adveniat regnum tuum,* Let us
338 Let us
341 [Biblical reference in margin] by way of Reproofe and Increpation] *You said,*
342 *over us;* Now, that was not their fault; but that which followes, The unseasonablesse
     and inconsideration of their clamorous Petition, *You said a King shall reigne over us*
346 a thing good in it selfe, and a good intended to them

9

ther tie, god his tyme, ~~and~~ ther would not stay
his leasure; and ~~bidd them~~ both their to aske other
thinges then god would giue, or at other
tymes then god would giue them to dis-
pleasing to him. w[i]t[h] his meanes and..
stay his Loysure. But yet though god were Data.
displeasd with them, he executed his owne
purpose; he was angry with their manner
of asking a king but yet he gaue them a
king. Howsoever god be displeasd with
them that probaritate in his cause, we
should sustayne him, and do not, Goodd cause
shall be sustaind, though they do it not.
we may distinguish the period of the Dow-
ith state well inough, thus. That they had
Infantiam or pueritiam, their infancy
their Minoritie in Adam, and his first
Patriarkes till the flood; That they had
Adolescentiam a growing tyme, from
Noah through the later Patriarkes, till
Moses. That they had Juuentutem, a
youth and strenght from Moses
through

they fix god his tyme, ~~and~~ ^{they} would not stay 347

*

his leasure; and ~~bide there~~ **both these,** to aske other 348

things then god would giue, or at other 349

tymes then god would giue them is dis= 350

pleasing to him. vse his means and 351

stay his leysure. But yet though god were   *Data.* 352

displeasd with them, he executed his owne 353

purpose; he was angry with their manner 354

of asking a King but yet he gaue them a 355

King. Howsoeuer god be displeasd with 356

them that prevaricate in his cause, who 357

should sustayne him, and do not, Gods cause 358

shall be sustaind, though they do it not. 359

we may distinguish the period of the Iew= 360

ish state well inough, thus. That they had 361

Infantiam or pueritiam, their infancy, 362

their Minoritie in Adam, and the first 363

Patriarchs till the flood; That they had 364

Adolescentiam a growing tyme, from 365

Noah through the later Patriarchs, till 366

Moses. That they had *Iuuentutem,* a 367

youth and strength from *Moses* 368
through

---

347   *fixed . . .* and they
348   either of these
352M   *Dabat.*
357   who
358   it
366   other
367   and that

through the Judges to ~~Paul~~ _{Saul} But then they)
had virilitatem, virilem ætatem, their
established vigor under their Kings: and
after them, they were in Senectute, in a
wretched and miserable decay of old age.
Their Kingdome was their best state.
And that, god in the prophet intimates
pregnantly, when representing unto their
Memories, in a particular Inventary, and
Ezech:
16.13.
Catalogue, all his former benefitts to them,
how he clothed Jerusalem, how he fedd her
how he beautified her, he sums up all in
his one, Et profecisti in regnum, & have
advanced thee to be a Kingdome. There
was the Tropique, there was the Solstice,
farther then it, in this world, we knowe
not how god could goe; a Kingdome
was really, the best state upon earth, and
Symbolically, the best figure, and type
of heaven. And therefore when the
prophet Jeremie historically, beheld the
declination of his Kingdome in the death
of Josiah, and prophetically foresaw
the ruine thereof in the transportation

of

              d   *Saul*

through the Iuges to ~~saue~~. But then they   369

had *virilitatem, virilem* <u>*ætatem*</u>, their   370

establishd vigor, vnder their Kings: and   371

after them, they <u>were in *Senectute,* in</u> a   372

wretched and miserable decay of old <u>age</u>.   373

Theyr kingdome was their best state.   374

And <u>that</u>, god in the prophet intimats   375

pregnantly, when refreshing <u>vnto</u> theyr   376

Memories, in a particular Inventary, and   377

Ezech: Catalogue, all his former benefitts to them,   378
16.13.

how he clothd Ierusalem, how he fed her,   379

how he <u>beutified</u> her, he sumd vp all in   380

this one, <u>*Et* profecisti in regnum</u>, I haue   381

aduancd thee to be a kingdome. There   382

was the Tropique, there was the Solstice;   383

farther then <u>it</u>, in this world, we knowe   384

not how god could goe; a kingdome   385

was really the best state vpon earth, and   386

Symbolically the best figure, and Tipe   387

of heauen. And therefore when the   388

prophet *Ieremie* historically beheld the   389

declination of this kingdome in the death   390

of *Iosiah*, and prophetically foresaw   391

the <u>ruine</u> thereof in the <u>transportion</u>   392
                      of

---

370   *atatem*
372   fell *in senectutem,* into
373   age, and decrepitnesse
375   so much
376   to
378M *Ezek.16.3.*
380   adorned
381   &
384   that
392   ruines . . . transportition

of Zedechiah, or, if he had foone Meat-
Historically too, yet prophetically, he fore=
saw the utter devastation, and depo=
pulation, and extermination, which
scatterd that nation soone after to this, to
his day, and God, and no man, knowes
how long, when they, who were a Kig=
dome, are nowhere a village, and they,
who had such Kings have nowhere a
Constable of their own. Historically, pro=
phetically, Jeremie had just cause of
Lamentation for the danger of that
Kingdome.

we had so also, for this our Kingdome, his
day. God hath given us a Kingdome,
not as other Kingdomes, made upp of
divers Cittyes, but of divers Kingdomes.
And all these Kingdomes were destind by
them to desolation in one minute. It
was not onely the destruction of the
present persons, but of the Kingdome;
for to submitt the Kingdome to a
forreine prelate, was to destroy the
Monarchy, to annihilate the Supremine,
to

*

of *Zedechiah*, or, if he had seene ~~it~~that   393

historically too, yet prophetically he fore=   394

saw the vtter devastation, and depo=   395

pulation, and extermination, which   396

scatterd that nation soone after Christ, to   397

this day, and god, and no man, knowes   398

<u>how long</u>, when they, who were a king=   399

nowhere
dome, are ~~now here~~ a village, and they,   400

nowhere
who had such kings haue ~~now here~~ a   401
ʌ

Constable of their own, historically, pro=   402

phetically, *Jeremie* had iust cause of   403

lamentation for the danger of that   404

Kingdome.   405

we had so also, for this our kingdome, this   406

day. God hath giuen vs a kingdome,   407

not as other kingdomes, made vpp of   408

diuers Cittyes, but of diuers kingdomes.   409

And all <u>these</u> kingdomes were destind <u>by</u> 410

<u>them to</u> Desolation in one minute. It   411

was not onely the destruction of the   412
<u>present</u>
~~great~~ <u>persons</u>, but of the kingdome;   413
ʌ

for to submitt the kingdome <u>to a</u>   414

foreine prelate, was to destroy the   415

Monarchy, to annihilate the Supremicie,   416
                                                  to

---

399   for how long
400   now no where
401   now no where
410   those
410–11   to
413   *persons present*
414   to the government of a

to ruine the verie forme of the king=
dome; a kingdome under another head
beside the king, is not a kingdome, about
it. The oath that the Emperour takes to
the Pope, is by them autors called Juramen=
tum fidelitatis an oath of Allegeance,
and if they had brought our king to take
an oath of Allegeance so, this were no
kingdome; Pope Nicolas 2 went about
to create 2 kingdomes, that of Tuscan
and that of Lombardy: his successors
have gone about to destroy many, for to
make it depend upon him, were to ..
destroy our kingdome. That they have
have attempted historically; and as long
as these Axioms and these Aforesaid
remaine in their Autors, that one sayth,
All christian kingdomes are de jure helds
of the Pope, and are de facto forfeited
to the Pope And other sayth, Christendome
would be better governed, if the Pope
would take the forfeiture, and take all
these royall farmes into his own demesne;
we see also their prophetirall desire, ..
their prophetirall intention, against the
kingdome

to ruine the verie forme of <u>the</u> king= 417

dome; a kingdome vnder another head 418

<u>beside</u> the king, is not a kingdome, as ours 419

is. The oath that the Emperour takes to 420

the Pope, is by theyr autors calld *Juramen=* 421

tum fidelitatis an Oath of Allegeance, 422

and if they had brought our kings to take 423

*   an oath of Allegeance so, this were no 424

* ------   kingdome; Pope Nicolas <u>2</u> went about 425

------   to create 2 kingdomes, That of *Tuscan*, 426

and that of *lombardy*: his successors 427

haue gone about to destroy <u>many</u>; for to 428

make it depend vpon him, were to 429

destroy our kingdome. That they ~~haue~~ 430

haue attemted historically; and as long 431

as these Axioms <u>and these</u> Aforisms 432

remaine in their Autors, that one <u>says</u>, 433

<u>All christian kingdomes are *De Jure* held</u> 434

of the Pope, and <u>are *De facto* forfeited</u> 435

             an

*   to the <u>Pope</u> And ^other <u>says</u>, Christendome 436

would be better governd, if the Pope 437

would take the forfeiture, and <u>take</u> all 438

these royall farmes into his own demesne, 439

we see also their propheticall desire, 440

their propheticall intention, against this 441
                        kingdome

---

417   a
419   besides
425   *the second*
428   more
432   and
433   shall say
434   that *De jure*, by right all Christian kingdomes doe hold
435   *De facto*, are forfeited
436   Hope . . . shall say, that
438   so bring

knigdome, what they would do. In their
Actions we have their History, and in their
Axions the prophesy.

Jeremie lamented the desolation of the
knigdome, but expressed in the deathe and
destruction of the king. He did not divide
the king and the knigdome, as if the kingdome could be well and the king in dis-
tres. *Omnipotentia Dei asylum hæ-*
reticorum; it is well said by more
then one of the Antients the omnipo-
tence of god, is the Sanctuary of all
heretiqus: when they would establish any
heresy, they fly to gods Almightines;
God can do all therefore he can do this.
So they establish their heresy of Transub-
stantiation, so they deliverance of Souls
not onely from purgatory, but from
Hell it selfe. They thinke to stopp all
mouthes with that, God can do it, no man
dares deny that; when if that were graunted everie in hand, things imply contradiction in themselfs, or contradiction to gods
word, cannot be graunted, god can not do
that, for god cannot ly. yet therefore
                        can

Regnum
in Rege.

kingdome, what they would do. In their   442

Actions we haue <u>the</u> history, and in their   443

Axioms <u>the</u> prophecy.   444

Jeremie lamented the desolation of the   *Regnum*   445

kingdome, <u>but</u> expressd in the Death and *in Rege.* 446

Destruction of the king. He did not diuide   447

the king and the kingdome, as if the king=   448

dome could <u>be</u> well and the king in dis=   449

tres. *Omnipotentia Dei asylum Hæ=*   450

reticarum; it is well said by more   451

then one of the Ancients <u>The</u> omnipo=   452

tence of god, is the Sanctuary <u>of all</u>   453

Heretiqus: when they would establish any   454

heresy, they fly to gods Almightines;   455

God can do all, therefore he can do this.   456

<u>So</u> they establish their heresy of Transub=   457

stantiation, <u>so</u> theyr deliverance of Souls   458

<u>not onely from purgatory</u>, but from   459

Hell it selfe. They thinke to stopp all   460

Mouthes with that, God can do it, no man   461

dares deny that; <u>when</u>, if that were graun=   462

ted (which, in <u>things, which imply</u> contra=   463

diction in themselfs, or contradiction to gods   464

word, cannot be graunted, <u>god</u> can ᵔdo   465

that, <u>for god</u> cannot ly) yet though\
        can   466

443 their
444 we have their
446 but that,
449 do
452 that the
453 of
457 So, in the *Roman Church,*
458 And so
459 not from *Purgatory* onely
462 when as
463 such things, as naturally imply
465 for God
466 God

ran do yt, concludes not that god will do yt, or cate doome it. Omnipotentia dei Asylum Hæreticorum, And so Salus regni Asylum proditorum, Great treasons and seditions, and rebellions haue never been set on foote, then vpon color and pretense off a care off the state, and the good off the kingdome. Euery where the king is Sponsus regni, the husband off the kingdome; and to make loue to the kings wife, and vndertake him, must needs make any king ealous. The king is Anima regni, the Soule off the kingdome; and to prouide for the health off the body, by the detriment off the Soule, is yll physick. The king is Caput regni, the head off the kingdome, and to cure a member, by cutting off the head, is yll Surgery; Man and wife, Soule and body, Head and Members, god hate ioyned, and ~~ffe~~ whome god hate ioyned let no man seuer: Salus regni asylum proditorum. To pretend to vphold the kingdome, and ouer throw the king hate euer been his tentation before,

                                                  and

can do yt, concludes not that god will do 467

yt, or hath donne it. *Omnipotentia dei,* 468

Asylum Hæreticorum, And so *Salus* 469

regni, *Asylum proditorum,* Gᵉrater 470

treasons, and seditions, and rebellions 471

haue neuer been set on foote, then vpon 472

color and pretence of a care of the state, 473

and the good of the kingdome. Euery 474

where the king is *Sponsus regni,* The 475

husband of the kingdome; and to make 476

loue to the kings wife, and vnderva= 477

lew him, must needs make any king iealous. 478

The king is *Anima regni,* The Soule 479

of the kingdome; and to prouide for the 480

health of the body, by the detriment of 481

the Soule, is yll phisick. The king is 482

Caput regni, the head of the kingdome, 483

and to cure a member, by cutting of 484

the head, is yll Surgery. Man and 485

wife, Soule and body, Head and Mem= 486

bers, god hath ioynd, and ~~therefore~~ those whome 487

god hath ioynd let no man seuer: *Salus* 488

regni asylum proditorum, To pretend to 489

vphold the kingdome, and ouer throw the 490

king hath euer been the tentation before, 491
and

---

467 God *can*
469 *Asylum hæriticorum,* The omnipotency of God, is the Sanctuary of Heretiques
470 *Regni,* is
474 and of
478 necessarily
481 with
482 perverse
484 off

12

and the vertue after in the greatest Grea=
sons. In that Action of the Iews, wgine we
nistiked vpon before, in theyr procedinge
for a king. The Elders of Israel gathered   1Sam:
together, So far they were in theyr way;   8
for this was no popular no seditious
assembly of light and turbulent Men;
but the Elders: and then they came to Sa=
muel; so far they were in theyr right
way too: for they colde not take right apart,
but came to the right place for redresse
of greivances, to theyr then chiefest go=
vernour, to Samuel. vpon they were
then lawfully met, they forbear not
to lay open puto him, the innumsities of
gis officers, though it concerned the very
Sonns of Samuel: and thus far they
kept within convenient limitts: but
wgen they would presse Samuel to a
new way of remedy, to an inconvenient
way, to a present way, to theyr own
way and nothing noteniny to him, wgat care
soever they pretended of the good of the state,

it

and the excuse after in the greatest trea=   492

*

sons. In th**at** Action of the Iews, which we   493

insisted vpon before, in theyr pressinge   494

for a king. The elders of Israel <u>gatherd</u>   495

togeather, <u>So</u> far they were in theyr way;   *1 Sam:*   496
8

for this was no popular, no seditious   497

assembly of light and turbulent Men;   498

but the elders: and then they came to *Sa*=   499

muel; <u>so</u> far they were in theyr right   500

way too. for they held <u>not</u> counsayls apart,   501

but came to the right place, for redresse   502

of greivances, to theyr then highest go=   503

vernor, to *Samuel*. when they were   504

<u>then</u> lawfully met, they forbear not   505

to lay open vnto him, the <u>iniustices</u> of   506

his <u>officers</u>, though it concernd the very   507

Sonns of *Samuel*: and thus far they   508

kept <u>within</u> convenient limitts: but   509

when they would presse *Samuel* to a   510

new way of remedy, to an inconuenient   511

way, to a present way, to theyr own   512

way and refer nothing to him, what care   513

soeuer they pretended of the good of the state,   514
it

---

495   were *gathered*
496   and so
500   And so
501   no
505   thus
506   injustice
507   greatest Officers
509   within their

it is euident that they had no good opi=
nion of Samuel: and even that dis=
pleased god, to be yll affected to the per=
son whome he had set over them. To
sever the king and the kingdome,
and pretend the weale of the one, with
out the other, is to shake, and distinguish
gods buildinge.

Historically this was the Iews case, when Iere=
mie lamented here, if he lamented the decli=
nation of that state, in the deathe of the kinge
Iosiah, And if he lamented the transportation of
Zedeckiah, and that that were not yet come, or
if he lamented the deuastation of that nation
occasioned by the deathe of the king of kings
Christ Iesus himselfe, when he came, this
was their case prophetically. Either way,
historically or prophetically, Ieremie looke
vpon the kingdome through that glasse, through
the king. The dutye of the day, and the or=
der of the text invites vs to an application
of this crowne too. our aduersaries did not
come to say to him selfe, Nolumus reg=
num hoc we will not have this kingdome
                                                    stand

Luc
19·14·

it is euident that they had no good opi=   515

nion of _Samuel_; and even that dis=   516

pleased god, <u>to be</u> yll affected to <u>the</u> per=   517

son whome he had set over them. To   518

seuer the king and the kingdome,   519

and pretend the Weale of the one, with   520

out the other, is to shake, and discompose   521

gods buildinge.   522

Historically this was the Iews case, when _Jere=_   523

mie lamented here, if he lamented the Decli=   524

nation of <u>that</u> state, in the Death of the kinge   525

Josiah, And if he lamented the transportation of   526

Zedechiah, and <u>that that</u> were not yet <u>come</u>, or   527

if he lamented the <u>deuastation</u> of that nation   528

occasioned by the death of the king of kings   529

* Christ Iesus himselfe, when he came, this   530

was their case prophetically. Eyther way,   531

historically, or prophetically, _Jeremie_ looks   532

vpon the kingdome <u>through</u> that glasse, Through   533

the king. The duety of the day, and the or=   534

der of the text inuites vs to an application   535

of this branch too. Our aduersaries did not   536

come to say to them selfes, _Nolumus reg=_   537

luc
_19.14._ _num hoc_ we will not haue this kingdome   538

stand

---

516   _Samuel_ himself
517   That they were . . . that
525   the
527   that that crosse . . . come upon them
528   future devastation
530   Christ Jesus, when he came into the world
533   but yet through
538M   _14.14_

13

stand; the materiall kingdome, the plenty of the
~~kingdome~~ land, they would have been content to have,
but the formall kingdome, that is his forme
of gouerment, by a Soueraine King that depends vpon none but god, they would not have.
So that they (implicitly) to Nolumus regnum --
hoc, we will not have this kingdome to be
gouernd thus, and explicitly for Nolumus regem
hunc, we will not have this King to gouerne
vs at all. Non hunc? will you not have him?
you were at your Nolumus have long before,
you would not have that ~~grant~~ to raigne
ouer you. There, your, not aminersary, but
(ordinary) treason rast vpon him a necessi-
tie of drawing blood often: and so your Nolumus have might have some ground. But
your Nolumus hunc, for this King, who --
had made no Inquisition for blood, who --
had forborne his very pecuniary penalties, who had
(as himselfe witnesse of himselfe) made
you partakers, with him Subiects of his
own religion, in matters of grace, in wall
bounties,

stand, the materiall kingdome, the plenty of the 539
land
~~kingdome~~, they would haue been content to haue, 540
∧

but the formall kingdome, that is this forme 541

of gouerment, by a Soueraine king that de= 542

pends vpon none but god, they would not haue. 543
came
So that that they implicitly to *Nolumus regnum* 544
∧

hoc, we will not haue this <u>kingdome to be</u> 545
to a
gouernd thus, <u>and</u> explicitely *Nolumus regem* 546
∧

hunc, we will not haue this king to gouerne 547

<u>vs at all</u>. *Non hunc?* will you not haue him? 548

you were at your *Nolumus hanc* long before, 549
Queene
<u>you would not haue that ------- to raigne</u> 550
∧

<u>ouer you</u>. <u>There, your</u>, not aniuersary, but 551

hebdomidary treasons cast vpon her a necessi= 552

tie of drawing blood often: and so your <u>*No*=</u> 553

<u>*lumus hanc*</u> might haue some <u>ground</u>. But 554

<u>your</u> *Nolumus hunc*, for this king, who 555

had made no Inquisition for blood, who 556
penalties,
had forborne <u>the</u> very pecuniary, who had 557
∧

(as himselfe witnesses of himselfe) made 558

you partakers, with his Subiects of his 559

own religion, in matters of grace, <u>in</u> reall 560
benefits,

---

545   Kingdome
546   and they came
547   *hunc* (as the Jewes were resolved of Christ)
548   at all
550–51 Her, whom God had set over you, before him, you would not have
551   Your
553–54 *Nolumus hanc*, your desire that she were gone, . . . kinde of ground, or colour
555   for your
557   your
560   and in

benefitt, and in titles of honor, Quare fre-
muerunt, why did these Men rage, and
imagine a vayne thinge? what they did historically we knew: they made that house
wherin is the throne of this kingdome, from
whence all her thinge comes, that house, where
Justice her selfe is conveyed, in their preparing
of good lawes, and maiminated and quirkned
and borne by the royall assent then given,
they made that whole house, one Murdering
peece: and hauing put in their powder,
they reared that peece with peeres, with ---
people, with princes, with the king, and
ment to discharg it vpward at the face of
heauen, to shoote god at the face of god him
of whome god had sayd, Dij estis, you are
gods, at the face of that god who had said
so: as though they would haue reproved the
god of heauen, and not haue been beholden
to him for such a king, but shoote him vp
to him and bid him take his king a
gaine

(margin) Psal:
2.1.

benefits, and in titles of honor, *Quare fre=* 561

psa:
2.1. *muerunt,* why did these Men rage, and 562

imagine a vayne thinge? what they did histo= 563

rically we know: They made that House 564

which is the hyue of ~~of~~ <u>this</u> kingdome, from 565

whence all her Hony comes, That House, where 566

Justice herselfe is conceyud, in their preparing 567

of <u>good laws</u>, and inanimated and quickned 568

and borne by the Royall assent <u>then</u> giuen, 569

they made that whole house, one Murdring 570

peece: <u>and hauing put in theyr powder,</u> 571

<u>they chargd</u> that peece with Peers, with 572

people, with Princes, with the King, and 573

* ment to discharg it vpward at the face of 574

heauen, to shoote god at the face of god, Him, 575

of whome god <u>had</u> sayd, *Dij estis,* you are 576

* gods, at the face of <u>that god who</u> had said 577

so: as though they would haue reprochd the 578

god of heauen, and not haue been beholden 579

to him for such a king, but shoote him vp 580

to him and bid him take his king <u>a</u> 581
gaine

565	the
568	*Laws*
569	there
571–72	and charged
576	hath
577	God, that

againe, for *Nolumus hunc regnare*, we
will not haue this king to reigne ouer vs.
T giue their case Historically, and what
it is prophetically, as longe as that remains
their doctrine, requir ed, against whome
that attempt was principally made, found
by theyr Examinations to be theyr doctrine,
That they, and no sort in the worlde, but they,
did make treason an article of religion,
That theyr religion bound them to these at=
tempts, so long they are neuer at an end;
till they disauow these doctrines, that con=
duce to yt, prophetically, they wish, prophe=
tically they hope for better successe in
worse attempts.

It is then the kingdome that Ieremie lamentb:
but this nearest object is the king: Et   **Rex**
monts enn. first, that it be, as with Hie=   **bonus**
rome, many of the Antients, and with them
Many of the later rabbins, will haue it for
Iosias, for a good king, in whose death
the honor and strength of that kingdome,
tooke that deadly wound, to be come tri=
butarie

againe, for *Nolumus hunc regnare*, we 582

will not haue this king to reigne ouer vs. 583

This was our case historically, and what 584

it is prophetically, as longe as that rer..ains 585

their doctrine, which he, against whome 586

that attempt was principally made, found 587

by theyr Examinations to be theyr doctrine, 588

That they, and no sect in the world but they, 589

did make treason an article of Religion, 590

That theyr Religion bound them to those at= 591

tempts, so long they are neuer at an end; 592

tyll they disauow those Doctrines, that con= 593

duce to yt, prophetically they wish, prophe= 594

tically they hope for better successe in 595

worse attempts. 596

It is then the kingdome that *Ieremie* laments: *Rex* 597

but his nearest obiect is the king: he la= *bonus* 598

ments him. first, let it be, as with *Hie=* 599

rome, many of the Ancients, and with them 600

Many of the later Rabbins, will haue it, for 601

Iosias, for a good king, in whose death 602

the honor and strength of that kingdome, 603

tooke that deadly wound, to be come tri= 604
butarie

581–82   again, with a
586   to bee their
588   examination
594   that
596   as ill
597–98M: [omitted in F50]
599–600   S. *Hierome*
603   the strength . . . the

butary) to a forrane prince: for to his -
lamentation, they refer, these wordes, which

Zecha: 12.11. describe a great sorrowe, In that day, shall
there be a great mourninge in Ierusalem
at the mourninge of Hadradrimmon .
in the valley of Megiddon; which was the
place where Iosiah was slaine, there
shall be sure a lamentation, as was for
Iosiah. This then was for him, for a
good king. wherein have we his goodnes
expressed? Abundantly, He did that which
was right in gods ey sight. And who so by-
needes he feare, that is right in the ey of god?

2 reg: 22.2 but how longe? To the end - for Nero who
had his _Quinquennium_, was worst of all.
he that is yll all the way, is but a Tirant,
he that is good at first, and after yll. An
Angels face, and a Serpents tayle make
him a monster. Iosiah persevered; he
turned not aside to the right hand, nor
to the left. As we applie it to the Iosiah
of our tyme, neither to the fugitive, that
leaves

butary to a foraine prince: for to this　　605

lamentation, they refer, those <u>words</u>, which　　606

Zecha 12.11. describe a great sorrowe, In that day, shall　　607

there be a great mourninge in *Jerusalem*　　608

as the mourninge of <u>Hadradrimmon</u>.　　609

in the valley of *Megiddon*; which was the　　610

place, where *Josiah* was slaine, There　　611

shall be such a <u>lamentation,</u> as was <u>for</u>　　612

Josiah; This then was for him; for a　　613

good king. wherein haue we his goodnes　　614

expressd? Abundantly. He did that which　　615

was right in gods ~~ey~~ sight. And whose Ey　　616

<u>needs</u> he fear, that is right in the ey of god?　　617

2 reg 22.2 but how <u>longe</u>? To the end. for *Nero* who　　618

*　 had his <u>Quinque**nnium,** was</u> worst of all.　　619

He that is yll all the way is but a <u>Tirant,</u>　　620

he that is good at first, and after yll, An　　621

Angells face, and a Serpents tayle make　　622

*　 him a monster; *Josiah* <u>perseuerd;</u> He　　623

turned not <u>a side</u> to the right hand, nor　　624

to the left. <u>If</u> we applie it to the *Josiah*　　625

of our <u>tyme</u>, neither to the fugitiue, that　　626
　　　　　　　　　　　　leaues

606　words of the Prophet
609　*Hadadrimmon*
612　lamentation (says the Prophet, in this interpretation) . . . for the death of
617　need
618　long did he so
619　*Quinquennium,* and was a good Emperour for his first five years, was one of the
620　*Tyran*
623　began well, and persevered so
624　*aside*
625　That is, (if
626　times

loaued our Churre, and good to hys Romans,   15

nor to hys Separatist, that loaued our ~~

Churre, and good to none. In the eighteenth

year of his reigne, he undertooke the repa=

ration of good house. If we applie that

to the Josiah of our tymes, & thinke in

that year of his reigne, he visited these

walls. In one word like to him there was

no king before, nor after. and therefore   23.25.

there was iust cause of Lamentation for

his King; for Josiah; Exoterically; for

the very losse of his person, Propheti=

rally; for the misery of the state, after

his death.

Our errand is to day, to applie all these

braunces to the day. These men who intended

as this cause of Lamentation this day, in

the destruction of our Josiah, spared

him not, because he was so, because he

was a Josiah, because he was good.

No, not because he was good to them; his

benefitts to them, had not mollified them

to him

leaues our Church, and goes to the Romane, 627

nor to the Separatist, that leaues our 628

Church, and goes to none. In the eighteenth 629

year of his reigne, <u>he</u> vndertooke the repa= 630

ration of gods house; If we applie <u>that</u> 631

to the *Josiah* of our tymes, I thinke in 632

that year of his reigne, he visited <u>these</u> 633

<u>walls</u>. In one word, like <u>to him</u> there was 634

no king before, nor after; and therefore   23.25. 635

there was iust cause of lamentation for 636

this king; for *Josiah*; historically, for 637

the very losse of his person, propheti= 638

cally, for the misery of the state, after 639

his death. 640

Our errand is to day, to applie all these 641

branches to the day. Those men who intended 642

vs this cause of lamentation this day, in 643

the destruction of our *Josiah*, spard 644

him not, because he was so, because he 645

was a *Josiah*, because he was good. 646

No, not because he was good to them, his 647

benefitts to them, had not mollified them 648
                            to him

---

630   *Josiah*
631   this
633–34 *this Church, and these wals, and meditated, and perswaded the reparation thereof*
634   *unto Josiah,*

to Emñ. for that ys not their way. bote the
strong Henries were their own, good to them;
and did that refeus vyseor of them, from the
knife? and was not that Emperour who they)
presonte in the Sacrament, theyr owne, and
good to them; And was that any Antidote
agaynst theyr poyson? To so reprobate a
sense hath god gewen them over, as that, though
they by examiost in theyr booke, vpon prim-
ses of our religion, yet truly, they haue
destroyd more of theyr owne, then of ours.
Thus it ys historirally, in theyr proceeding
past, and prophetirally, yt ran be but theys,
ffirst no king ys good, in theyr sense, if he
not
agree to all poynts of doctrine with them, and
when that ys donne, not good yet, except he
aigree in all poynts of Jurisdiction too; and that
no king ran doo, that will not be theyr far-
mer of his owne kingdome. Theyr autors haue
putted
disputed Auferibilitatem papæ; They)
haue

to him. for that is not their way. both the 649

French *Henries* were their own, good to them; 650

and did that rescue eyther of them, from the 651

knife? and was not that Emperour who^m they 652

* poysond in the Sacrament, theyr own, and 653

* good to them; And was that any Antidote 654

against theyr poyson? To so reprobate a 655

sense hath god giuen them over, as that, though 656

they ly heauiest in theyr books, vpon prin= 657

ces of our religion, yet truly they haue 658

* destroyd more of theyr owne, then of ours. 659

Thus it is Historically in theyr proceedings 660

past, and prophetically, yt can be but thus, 661

since no king is good, in theyr sense, if he 662

agree^not to all poynts of Doctrine with them, and 663

when that is donne, not good yet, except he 664

agree in all poynts of Iurisdiction too; and that 665

no king can doe, that will not be theyr far= 666

* mer of his owne kingdome. Theyr autors haue 667

* dis~~posed~~ **puted** *Auferibilitatem Papæ*; They 668
haue

---

649 towards
650 and good
651 but
654 and yet
656 over herein
657 in their *Books*, they ly heaviest
667 of his

16

haue made it a probleme, whether the degree
of god might not be without a Hope, and some
of theyr authors haue diuerted towards an af-
firmation of yt. but Auferibilitas potestatis,
to imagine a king without kingly Soueraim-
ty; neuer came into probleme, into disqui-
tation. we all lamented, and bitterly, and
iustly the losse of our Deborah. (once)
then were all saw a Josiah succeeding.
but if this had redeemed our Josiah..
and his children, and theyr forme of gouernment, where, or why, or what had been
an object of consolation vnto vs?

The cause of lamentation in the losse of a good
king is certainly, great; so it was, if

Lex
Malus.

Jeremie lamented Josiah; but if it were
but for Zedechiah an yll king (as the greater part of Expositors take it) yet the
lamentation we see is the same. How yll
a king was Zedechiah? very yll; as yll
as.

haue made it a Probleme, whether the Church 669

of god might not be with out a Pope, and some 670

of theyr autors haue diuerted towards an af= 671

firmation of yt. but *Auferibilitas potestatis*, 672

to imagine a king without kingly Souerain= 673

ty, neuer came into probleme, into dispu= 674

tation. we all lamented, and bitterly, and 675

iustly the losse of our *Deborah*, though 676

then <u>wee all</u> saw a *Josiah* succeeding: 677

but if <u>this</u> had re~~duced~~ our *Josiah* 678
                mou'd

and his <u>Children, and</u> this forme of gouer= 679

ment, where, or who, or what had been 680

an obiect of consolation <u>vnto</u> vs? 681

The cause of lamentation, in the losse of a good *Rex* 682
                                                       Malus.

king is cert**ai**nly great; <u>so</u> it was, if 683

Jeremie lamented *Josiah*; but if it were 684

but for *Zedechiah* an yll king (as the grea= 685

ter part of Expositors take it) yet the 686

lamentation <u>we</u> see is the same. How yll 687

a king was *Zedechiah*? <u>very yll; as yll</u> 688
                             as

668–70   whether the Church of God might not be without a *Pope,* they have made a
           problematicall, a disputable matter
677   we
678   they
679   *Royall children,* and so
681   to
683   and so
687   you
688   As ill

as Josiah was good; there hath his measure,
for he did evyll in the sight of the Lord, according to all that Jehoiakim had donne: ther

2 reg: his Syn; by precedent, he sett the worst
24.19.   kings before him, and is as bad as they):

23: ult what had Jehoiakim donne? he had donne
evyll in the sight of the Lord according to
all that his fathers had donne. It is a great
and dangerous wickednes, weire is donne
upon protext of antiquitie. the religion of
our fathers, the Churche of our fathers, the
worshipp of our fathers, is a protext that
robers a great deale of Superstition. he
did evyll as his father, there was his comparative evyll; and his positive evyll in
particular was, that he humbled not him-

2. Chron: selfe to good prophets, to Jeremie speaking
36.12.   from the Mouth of the Lord, there was
irreligiousnes; And then he had broke
that oath, weire he had sworne by
v.13.   god, there was faithlesnes; And Lastly
he

*	as *Josiah* was good; ~~thers~~ thats his measure,	689
	<u>for he</u> did evyll in the sight of the lord, accor=	690
	ding to all that *Jehoiakim* had donne: <u>her's</u>	691
2 reg 24.19.	his <u>Syn; by precedent; he sets the worst</u>	692
	<u>kings before him, and is as bad as they.</u>	693
<u>*23:ult*</u>	<u>what</u> had *Jehoiakim* donne? He had donne	694
	evyll in the sight of the lord according to	695
	all that his fathers had donne. It is a great,	696
	<u>and</u> dangerous wickednes, which is donne	697
	vpon pretext of antiquitie. The religion of	698
	our fathers, the Church of our fathers, the	699
	worship of our fathers, is a pretext that	700
	colors a great deale of Superstition. He	701
	did evyll, as his fathers, there was his com=	702
	paratiue evyll; and his positiue evyll <u>in</u>	703
	<u>particular</u> was, That he humbled not him	704
2.<u>Chom</u>: 36.12.	selfe to gods prophets, to *Jeremie* speaking	705
	from the Mouth of the lord, There was	706
	irreligiousnes; And then he ~~had~~ broke	707
	<u>that</u> oath, which he had sworne by	708
v. 13.	god, there was <u>faithlesnes;</u> And lastly	709
	he	

690	*He*
691	*Here is*
692–93	sinne, sinne by precedent;
694M	*2 Reg.25.ult.*
694	*and what*
697	*and a*
703–04	(I meane his particular sinne)
705M	*Chr:*
708	*the*
709	*perfidiousnesse,* faithlesnesse

he stiffned his neck, and hardned his hart,
from turning to the Lord god off Israell
there was impossiblenes: Thus euyll
was Zedechia, Irreligious to god, trea=
cherous to Man Impossible in himselfe
and yet the state lamented him; Not his
spirituall defections, his Synns; for they
did not make themselues Iudges off those,
but they lamented the calamities off the
kingdome, in the losse eben off an yll king.

That Man must haue a large Comprehension
that shall aduenture to say, off any king he
is an yll king; He must knowe his office well
and his actions well, and the actions off other
princes too, who haue correspondence with
him, before he can say so: when Christ sayd
let your Communication be yea yea, and   Mat: 5
nay, nay, for whatsoeuer is more then   37
these, when it comes to swouring, that It
comoneth off evill, Saint ~~Hierome~~ Augustine doth
not vnderstand it off the evyll disposition
off

he stiffned his neck, and hardned his hart, 710

from turning to the <u>lord god</u> of *Israel* 711

There was impenitiblenes: Thus evyll 712

was *Zedechia* Irreligious to god, trea= 713

cherous to Man, Impenitible <u>in</u> himselfe 714

and yet <u>the state</u> lamented him; Not his 715

spirituall defections, <u>his Syns</u>; for they 716

did not make themselfes Iudges of <u>those</u>, 717

but they lamented the calamities of the 718

kingdome, in the losse, even of an <u>yll</u> king. 719

That Man must haue a large Comprehension 720

that shall aduenture to say, of any king He 721

is an yll king. He must know his office well 722

and his actions well, and the actions of other 723

princes too, who haue correspondence with 724

him, before he can say so. when Christ says 725

let your Communication be yea yea, and   *Mat:5* 726
                                                 37.
nay, nay, for whatsoeuer is more then 727

<u>these</u>, when it comes to swearinge, that 728
                    Augustine
commeth of evill, Saint ~~Ambrose~~ does 729
                    ^
not vnderstand <u>it</u> of the evyll disposition 730
                                            of

---

711 *Lord*
714 to
715 the State, and men truly religious in the State, the Prophet
716 by sinne
717 that
719 evill
728 *this*, (that is,
730 that

of the Man that sweareth, but of them who
will not beleeve him without swearinge.
Many tymes a prince departs from the exact
rule of his duty, not out of his own disposition to truth and cleareness, but to coun-
termyne vndermyners. That which dauid
sayd he speaks of god himselfe, Cum --
peruerso peruerteris, with the froward --
thou wilt shew thy selfe froward: God who
is of no froward nature may be made froward. with craftie neighbours a prince
will be craftie and porreanw false with
the false. Alas, to looke into no other profession but our own, how often do we excuse
dispensations, and pluraletyes, and Nonresi-
dences, with an omnes faciunt, I do but
as other Men of my profession do: Allow
a king but that, he does but as other kings
do, or but that, as their denyes put him to a
necessity to do, and you will not quickly call
a king an ill king: when god shall give
people for else sheep, and for nought, and
quod

Ifa: 18
26.

	of <u>the</u> Man that swears, but of them who	731
will not beleeue him without swearinge.		732
Many tymes a prince departs from the exact		733
rule of his duty, not out of his own indispo=		734
sition to truth and clearnesse, but to coun=		735
termyne vndermyners. That which Dauid		736

of <u>the</u> Man that swears, but of them who   731

will not beleeue him without swearinge.   732

Many tymes a prince departs from the exact   733

rule of his duty, not out of his own indispo=   734

sition to truth and clearnesse, but to coun=   735

termyne vndermyners. That which Dauid   736

* <u>says he speaks</u> of god himselfe, *Cum*   737

peruerso peruerteris, with the froward   738

psa: 18 26. thou wilt shew thy selfe froward: God who   739

is of no froward nature may be made fro=   740

ward. with craftie neighbours a prince   741

will be craftie, and perchance false with   742

the false. Alas, to looke into no other pro=   743

fession ~~then~~ ^{but} our own, how often do we excuse   744

* dispensations, and pluralityes, and Nonresi=   745

dencyes, with an *Omnes faciunt*, I do but   746

as other Men ~~do~~ of my profession do: Allow   747

a king but that, <u>he</u> does but as other kings   748

do, <u>or but that, as their doings</u> put him to a   749

necessity to do, and you will not <u>quickly</u> call   750

a king, an yll king. when god <u>sells</u> his   751

people for old shooes, and <u>for nought</u>, and   752
                                    giues

---

731   that
737   sayes in the eighteenth Psalme, *David* speaks, not of man, but
739M *Vers.26.*
748   *That he*
749   Nay, but this, *He does but as other Kings*
750   hastily
751   *gives*
752   *sells them for nothing*

18

gives his enemyes abundance, when god com=
maundd Abraham to sacrifice his own and onely
sonne, and his enemies gaue children at their
pleasure as Dauid speakes, to giue your
selfe the libertie of humane affections, that yo{w}
would thinke god an yll god: but yet they
are to him a royall priesthood, and a holy)
nation for all that, and all their teares are
in his bottle, and registred in his booke for
all that. when princes intermitt in some
thinges, the present benefit of their sub=
iects and confer fauours vppon others, giue
your selfe the liberty to iudg of princes
actions, weigh the affections of priuat men,
and you may thinke a king an yll king.
but yet we are to him as Dauid sayd
2 Samuel 19.12 his brethren, his bone,
his flesh, and so reputed by him. God
himselfe cannot stand shriges in a
naturall mans interpretation, nor
any king in a priuate mans. but
then how soone our aduersaries come to
rull

giues his enemyes abundance, when god com=   753

maunds *Abraham* to sacrifice his own and onely   754

sonne, and his enemies haue Children at their   755

pleasure as *Dauid* speakes, to giue your   756

selfs the libertie of humane affections, ~~that~~ yo^w 757

would thinke god an yll god: but yet they   758

are to him a royall Preisthood, and a holy   759

nation for all that, and all their tears are   760

in his bottle, and registred in his booke for   761

all that. when princes pretermitt in some   762

things, the present benefit of their Sub=   763

iects, and confer fauours vpon others, giue   764

your selfs the liberty to iudg of princes   765

actions, with the affections of priuat men,   766

and you may thinke a king an yll king.   767

but yet we are to him as *Dauid* says   768

2. Samuel 19.12. His brethren, his bone,   769

his flesh, and so reputed by him. God   770

himselfe, cannot stand vpright in a   771

*   naturall Mans interpretation, nor   772

any king in a priuate mans. but   773

then how soone our aduersaries come to   774
                                         call

---

753   at the same time, gives his and their
757   affection
758   but yet, for all this, his children
760   *Nation*
761   *bottles*
762   this
769   [Biblical reference in F50's margin] *2 Sam.19.12.*

rall kings, ill kings, wee see historically, when
they boast of having deposd kings Quia minus
vtiles, because another gate seemed to them fitter
for that governent, and wee see prophetically)
by alowinge those inditements and attainders
of kings which stand in their booke de Syndica=
tu, that that king that neglects his dutye his
glare, that overrides his prerogative with
out iust cause, that vexes his Subiects, nay,
that gives ymselfe to intemperate gouernig
for in his very particular, they restrane, that in
suy cases kings are als more in theyr mercy)
and Subiect to censure and correction.—
we proceed not so in censuring the actions of
kings. we say with Civil, in John. 1 . 12 . 56.
impium est dicere regi, inique agis. we re=
mit the iudgment of theyr action to god, where
they are secret, and if they were audious and
bad, yet we must endeavour to preserve theyr
persons, for here is danger in the losse, and
lamentation due to the losse, even of Zedechiah,
for

call kings, yll kings, wee see historically, when   775

they bôst of hauing deposd kings *Quia minus*   776
      a

vtiles, because <u>another</u> hath seemed to them fitter   777

for <u>that</u> gouerment, and wee <u>see</u> prophetically,   778

<u>by</u> alowinge those inditements and attainders   779

of kings which stand in their books *de Syndica*=   780

tu, That that king <u>that</u> neglects the dutys of his   781

<u>place</u>, That exercises his prerogative with   782

out iust <u>cause, that vexes his Subiects, nay</u>   783

that giues himselfe to intemperate hunting   784
              at
for in the very particular, they instance, that in   785

<u>such cases kings are as much in theyr mercy,</u>   786
and   r
~~and~~ <u>subiect to censure and corection</u>.   787
    ^   ^

we proceed not so in censuring the actions of   788

kings. we say with <u>*Ciril, in John 1.12.56.*</u>   789

impium est dicere regi, <u>inique agis</u>. we re=   790
*

mit the iudgment of <u>theyr action to god, where</u>   791

<u>they are secret, and if they were euident</u> and   792

bad, yet we must endeuour to preserve their   793

persons, for there is <u>danger</u> in the losse, and   794

<u>lamentation</u> due to the losse, even of *Zedechiah*,   795
                                                                          for

---

777   some other
778   the . . . see it
779   by their
781   which
782   place (and they must prescribe the duty, and judge the negligence too) That King
783   cause (and they must prescribe the Prerogative, and judge the cause,) That that King
       that vexes his Subjects, That that King
786–87 such cases, (and they multiply these cases infinitely) Kings are in their mercy, and
       subject to their censures, and corrections.
789   St. *Cyrill*
790   *Inique agis; It is an impious thing,* (in him, who is onely a private man, and hath
       no other obligations upon him) *to say to the King,* or *of the King, He governs not
       as a King is bound to do:*
791–92 those their actions, which are secret to God; and when they are evident
794   a danger
795   a lamentation

for euen sure, and vncti Domini, the anointed of the
Lord, And spiritus narium, the Breath of or nostrills.
first, the king vt Spiritus Narium, the breath Spiritus
of our Nostrills. furst, Spiritus, a name most Narium.
peculiarly, belonging to god. That blessed person
of the glorious Trinitie, whose office is it, to
          sinuate
convay, to insinuate, to applie to vs the mercies
of the father, and the Meritts of the sonne, is
called by this name, by the word of his Text, Spiri= Spiritus
tus, Ruach, euen the begining of the Crea= Sanctus.
tion. God had created heauen, and earth;
and then the Spirit of god, sufflabat, sayd
Hagnius translation, and so sayst the Vgalde
paraphrase, it breathed vpon the waters, and so
nidurd or doded particular, and Specifique
formes. So god had made vs a litle world
of our own, his Iland; he had given vs
heauen and earth, the truce of his gospell,
our earnest of heauen, and at the abundance
of the earth, a fruitfull hand; but then,
to vse it the Spirit of the Lord, to vse it
the breath of our Nostrills, Incubat aquis,
he moues vpon the waters, by this royall
                                        and

for euen such are vncti Domini, **the anointed of the** 796

Lord, And spiritus Narium, The Breath of oʳ Nostrills. 797

<u>First</u>, the king is *Spiritus Narium*, the breath   *Spiritus* 798
Narium.

of our Nostrills. first, *Spiritus;* a name most 799

peculiarly belonging <u>to god.</u> That blessed person 800

of the glorious Trinitie, whose office it is, to 801

$\overset{\textbf{sinuate}}{}$

conuay, to in~~treate~~, to applie to vs the mercies 802

of the father, and the Merits of the Sonne, <u>is</u> 803

calld by $\overset{this}{\text{~~that~~}}$ name, by the word of this Text, <u>*Spiri*</u>=   *Spiritus* 804

tus, <u>Ruach</u>, euen $\overset{in}{\text{the}}$ begining of the Crea=   *Sanctus.* 805

tion. God ha$\overset{d}{\text{th}}$ created heauen, and earth; 806

and then the Spirit of god, *sufflabat,* <u>says</u> 807

Pagnins translation, and so <u>says</u> the Chalde 808

<u>Paraphrasts</u>, it breathd vpon the waters, and so 809

inducd or deduc'd <u>particular, and specifique</u> 810

formes. So god hath made vs a litle world 811

of our own, this Iland; he hath giuen vs 812

heauen and earth, the truth of his ghospell, 813

<u>our</u> earnest of heauen, and ~~ab~~ the <u>abundances</u> 814

of the earth, a fruitfull land; but then, 815

he who is the Spirit of the lord, he who is 816

the breath of our Nostrills, <u>*Incubat aquis,*</u> 817

he moues vpon the waters, by his royal$\underset{and}{\text{l}}$ 818

797	*and*
798	First, (as it lies in our Text)
799	*Spiritus,* is
800	to
803	He is
804–05	*Ruach*
804–05M	[not in F50]
807	saith
808	saith
809	*Paraphrase* too
810	particular
814	which is our . . . abundance
817	*Incubat aquis,* (as it is said there in the Creation)

and warlike Nauy), at Sea, in w[hi]ch he hath ex=
presses a spe[ci]all, and a pa[r]ticular care, and
by the breath and influence of his prouidence
through out the land, he p[re]serues he applies, he
makes p[ro]fitable these the things vnto vs. As this
breath, that is his power, be at any ^time corrupt in his
passage, and contract an ill sauor, by the
pipes w[hi]ch conuay it, ^and his good intentions are
ill executed by inferior Magistrats, this
must not be imputed to him; That breath)
that comes from the East, the bed and harbor
of spices, is, when it is breathed out here, a
perfume; by passing ouer the bedds of Ser=
pents, and putrified lakes, it may be a
breath of poyson, in the west. p[ri]nces p[ur]=
pose somethinges for the ease of the people (and
as sure, they are sometymes represented to
them) and if they proue greiuances, they)
tooke theire putrifaction in the way, theyr
corruption from corrupt executors of
good intentions.

But here, we carry not his word, Ruach,
Spirit, so highe: hence, since god hath sayd,
that)

and warlike Nauy, at Sea, in which he hath ex=	819
pressd a speciall, and <u>a particular</u> care, and	820
by the breath and influence of his prouidence	821
throughout the land, he preserves, he applies, he	822
makes vsefull <u>these</u> blessings vnto vs. If this	823
breath, that is this power, be at any _^<u>corrupt</u> in the ^time	824
passage, and contract an yll Sauor, by the	825
pipes <u>which convay it,</u> his good intentions are **and**	826
yll executed by inferior Mynisters, this	827
must not be imputed to him; That breath	828
that comes from the East, the bed and <u>garden</u>	829
of spices, <u>is, when it is breathd out there,</u> a	830
perfume; <u>by</u> passing ouer the beds of Ser=	831
pents, and putrified lakes, it may be a	832
breath of poyson, in the West. princes pur=	833
pose somethings for <u>the ease of</u> the people (and	834
as such, they are sometymes presented to	835
them) and if they proue greiuances, they	836
tooke their putrifaction in the way, <u>theyr</u>	837
corruption from corrupt executors of	838
<u>good intentions.</u>	839
Spiritus But <u>here,</u> we carry not this word, *Ruach,*	840
Sermo. Spirit, so highe: though, since god hath sayd, that	841

820   particular
823   those
824   sourd
826   that convay it, so, as that
829   the garden
830   when it is breathed out there, is
831   but by
834   ease to
837   that is, their
839   good and wholesome intentions; The thing was good in the roote, and the ill cannot be removed in an instant.
840   then

20

that things are good, the attribute of the holy
ghost and his office, were it to apply to man, the
goodnes of god, belongs to things &c. God giues,
but they applie all blessings to vs. but here   Non ma=
we take the word literally), as it is in the text,   ledictio.
Ruach, Spirit, is the breath that we breath,
the lyfe, that we liue. the body is that I breath,
that life, and therefore that belongs to him.
first, our breath, that is, sermo, our speech.

Be faithfull vnto him, and speake good of his   Psa: 100.
name, is commaunded by Dauid of god. to
god amonstod, we are not faithfull, if wee
do not speake good of his Name. first there
is an internall thing in the hart. God looke
to it. the fole hath said in his hart, there   Psa: 14.
is no god; though he say it but in his hart   1.
yet he is a foole. for as wise as a politi=
tian would thinke him for saying it in his
hart and comminge no farther, yet euen
that is an ouert act with god, for god sees
the hart. the fole sayth in his hart, there   Psal:
is no god. And it is the fole that sayth   too.
                           in his

that kings are gods, The attribute of the Holy 842

ghost, and his office, which is to apply to Man, the 843

goodnes of god, belongs to kings <u>too</u>; God giues, 844

but they applie all blessings to vs. but here   *Non Ma=* 845
ledictio.

we take the word, literally, as it is in the Text, 846

Ruach, Spirit, is the breath that we breath, 847

the lyfe, that we live. The king is that o breath, 848

that life, and therefore that belongs to him. 849

first, our breath, that is, *Sermo*, our <u>Speech</u>. 850

Be faithfull vnto him, and speake good of his   *psa:100.* 851

name, is commaunded by *Dauid* of god. To 852

gods annointed, we are not faithfull, if wee 853

do not speake good of his Name. first, there 854

is an internall speech in the hart: <u>God looks</u> 855

to ɪt. The foole hath said in his hart, there   *psa: 14.* 856
1.

is no god; Though he say it but in his hart, 857

yet he is a foole. for as wise as a politi= 858

cian would thinke him for sayinge it in his 859

hart, and comminge no <u>farther</u>, yet euen 860

that is an ouert act with god, for god <u>sees</u> 861

the hart. The foole <u>says</u> in his hart, there   *psa:* 862
100.

is no god; And it is the foole that <u>says</u> 863
in his

---

844   also; for,
845M   [not in F50]
850   *speech* belongs to him
851M   [not in F50]
855   and God
856M   [not in F50]
860   further
861   seeth
862   that saith
863   saith

Jud:
19.30.

21.25.

Eccles:
10.20.

† Bene=
dictio.

hart, I would here were no king. that on=
ermous, that infamous tragedy of the leuite
Concubin. and her Murder, of which it is
sayd here, there was no such euel donne
nor seene before, sayd many things are e
donne, that are neuer seene; with that em=
phaticall addition, consider of it, aduise, and
say your mind, take this addition to, in his
dayes here was no king in Israel: if there
had been any king, but a Zedechiah, it wold
not haue been so. Curse not the king, not in thy
thought: for they are signes that broade
vppon the goods of oneanother, that induce
one another to reuenge ytt of god himselfe,
nant, and of god himselfe: for so the
prophet ioynes them, Esaye 8. 21. they
shall fret themselfs, and curse their king
and their god. he that beginns with one,
will proceede to the other.

Thus then then is it our breath; our breath
is god, our speach must be contained not ex=
pressed in his dishonor: not in misinterpretati=
ons of his actions. Jealousies in loue often
made

Jud:	<u>hart</u>, I would there were no king. That en=	864
19.30.	ormous, that infamous tragedy of the *leuits*	865
	<u>Concubin</u>. and her Murder, of which it is	866
	sayd there, There was no such <u>deed donne,</u>	867
	<u>nor seene</u> before, (and many things are	868
*	donne, <u>that</u> are neuer seene) with that Em=	869
<u>*21.25.*</u>	phaticall addition, consider of it, aduise, and	870
	say your mind, hath this addition to, In those	871
	dayes there was no king in *Israel*; If there	872
	had been any king, but a *Zedechiah*, it could	873
Eccles:	not haue been so. Curse **not** the king, not in thy	874
10.20.	thoughts: for they are synns that tread	875
	vpon the heels of one another, <u>that</u> induce	876
	one another, to conceyue yll of gods liuete=	877
	nant, and of god himselfe: for so the	878
	prophet <u>ioynes them, *Esaye 8.21.*</u> They	879
	shall fret themselfs, and curse theyr king	880
	and there god. he that <u>begins with</u> one,	881
	will proceede to the other.	882
<u>*Bene=*</u>	Thus then ~~then~~ he is our breath; our breath	883
<u>*dictio.*</u>	is his; our speech must be containd, not ex=	884
	pressd in his dishonor: not in misinterpretati=	885
	ons of his actions. Ialousies ~~m~~ haue often	886
	made	

864   in his heart
866   Concubins
867–68   *thing seen, nor done*
869   which
870M   [not in F50]
876   and that
879   joyneth them, [Biblical reference in margin]
881   beginneth with the
883M   [not in F50]

made, woman ys: (incredulity), suspitiousnes
ialousy in the subiect say, remoues ill offices
vpon seruices, otherwise not ys. we must not
speake ill; but our duety is not accomplished in
that abstinence; we must speake well. And
in these things which will not admitt a good
interpretation, we must be apt to remoue
the obliquitie and peruersnes of the act,
from him, who is the first mouer, to those
who are inferior instrumentes. In those ob=
ous opinions, which are postilated in the
Schooles, how god concurrs to the workinges
of second and subordinate causes, that opinion
ys, (I thinke) the most antient, that denies.
that god workes in the second cause, but onely
hath communicated to that, a power of wor=
king, and workes himselfe: This is not true;
god doth worke in every organ, and in every
particular action: But yet though he do worke
in all, yet is no cause of the obliquity, of the
peruersnes of any action; now varietly prin=
ces are not equall to god; they do not worke
in

made women yll: Incredulity, suspitiousnes, 887

ialousy in the subiect hath wrought ill effects 888

vpon princes, otherwise not yll. we must not 889

speake ill; but our duety is not accomplishd in 890

that abstinence; we must speake well. And 891

in those things which will not admitt a good 892

interpretation, we must be apt to remoue 893

the <u>obliquitie and peruersnes</u> of the act, 894

from him, who is the first mouer, to those 895

who are inferior instruments. In <u>those</u> di= 896

uers opinions, which are ventilated in the 897

Schoole, how god <u>concurrs</u> to the workinge 898

of second and subordinate causes, that opinion 899

ys, (I thinke) the most ancient, That denies 900

that god works in the second cause, <u>but onely</u> 901

<u>hath</u> communicated to <u>that</u>, a power of wor= 902

king and <u>rests</u> himselfe: This is not true; 903

god <u>doth</u> worke in euery Organ, and in euery 904

particular action: But yet though he do work, 905

in all, <u>he</u> is no cause of the obliquity, of the 906

* peruersnes of any action; now earthly prin= 907

ces are not equall to god; they do not <u>worke</u> 908
in

894	perversenesse and obliquity	
896	these	
898	*concurreth*	
901–02	but hath onely . . . it	
903	rest	
904	does	
906	yet hee	
908	so much as worke	

in particular actions; many tymes they com=
municate power to others, and rest themselfs,
and the power is from them, but the pervers=
nes is not. God doth worke, and is not gilty;
but princes do not so much as worke therein,
and therefore are excusable.

Preces.
They are our breath; our breath is theyrs, in good
interpretations of their actions and it is theyrs
especially in our prayers to almightie
God for them. espeiaaly The Apostle exhorts vs to pray).

1 Tmo:
2.1.
for sosomes first for all men in generall:
but in the first particular, that he descends
to, for kings: And both Theodoret and
Theophylact make that the onely reason, why
he did not name kings first, et non vide=
atur adulari: least he should seeme to flatter

Magoli=
ands.
kings. whether mankind it selfe, or kings
by whom Mankind is happie here, be to
be preferred in prayer, you see both
Theodoret and theophylat make it a
probleme. And these prayers were for
infidell kings, and for persecutinge kings:
for

*	in particular <u>actions</u>; many tymes they com=	909
	municate power to others, and <u>rest</u> themselfs;	910
	<u>and</u> the power is from them, but the <u>peruers</u>=	911
	<u>nes</u> is not. God does <u>worke, and</u> is not gilty:	912
	but princes do not so much as worke therein,	913
	and <u>therefore are excusable</u>.	914
	They are our <u>breath</u>; our breath is theyrs, in good	915
Preces.	interpretations of their actions, and it is theirs	916
	especially in our ~~actio~~ **especially** prayers to allmightie	917
	god for <u>them</u>. The Apostle exhorts vs to pray.	918
*	for whome? first for all men in generall:	919
1 Timo:	but in the first particular that he descends	920
2.1.	to, for kings: And both *Theodoret* and	921
	Theophylact make that the onely reason, why	922
	<u>he</u> did not name kings first, *vt non vide=*	923
	atur adulari: least he should seeme to flatter	924
Magoli=	kings. whether mankind it selfe, or kings	925
anus.	by whome Mankind is happie here, be to	926
*	**ferd** be ~~preserud~~ in prayer, you see both	927
	Theodoret and *Theophylact* make it a	928
	Probleme. And those <u>prayers</u> were for	929
	infidell kings, and for persecuting kings:	930
	for	

909		actions of instruments
910		rest wholly
911		and then
912–12		*perversenesse* of the action
912		work in ill actions, and yet
914		so may bee excusable; at least, for any cooperation in the evill of the action, though not for countenancing, and authorising an evill instrument; but that is another case
915		breath then
916M		[not in F50]
918		them
923		the Apostle
925M		[not in F50]
929		prayers, there enjoyned,

22

for even they were the breath of their Nostrills;
Theyr breath, their swore, their prayers
were due to them. But then, beloued, a man may
conuay a Satire into a prayer, a man may
make a prayer a libell: if the intention of
the prayer be not so muth to incline god to
giue these graces, to the king, as to tell the
world that the king wants these graces, it
is a libell. we say sometymes in scorne to
a Man, God helpe you, and god send you witt,
and herein, because it haue the sound of a
prayer, we call him foole. So we haue
bene some of late in obscure conuenticles,
institute certayne prayers That god would
keepe the king, and the prince in his re=
ligion. The prayer is allwayes good, allwayes
lawfull. but when that prayer is accompa=
nied with circumstances as hauing the king
and prince more declyning from that
religion, then even the prayer it selfe is
libellous and seditious. Saint paul
in

  their

for even <u>they</u> were the breath of ~~our~~ Nostrills;   931

                    i

Theyr breath, ~~ther~~ their speech, their prayers   932

were due to them. But then, beloued, a man may   933

*   conuay a Satir into a prayer, a man may   934

make a prayer a libel; if the intention of   935

the prayer be not so much, to incline god to   936

giue those graces, to the king, as to tell the   937

world that the king wants those graces, it   938

is a libell. we say sometymes in scorne to   939

a Man, God helpe you, and god send you witt,   940

and therein, though it haue the sound of a   941

prayer, we call him foole. So we haue   942

seene <u>some of late</u> in obscure conventicles,   943

institute certayne prayers, That god would   944

keepe the king, and the prince in <u>this</u> re=   945

ligion. The prayer is allways good, allways   946

vsefull. but when that prayer is accompa=   947

nied with circumstances as though the king   948

and <u>prince</u> were declyning from that   949

religion, then euen the prayer it selfe is   950

libellous and seditious. *Saint Paul*   951

                                 in

---

931   such Kings
943   of late, some
945   *the true*
949   the Prince

in that former place, apparrels a subiecte
prayer well, when he sayd, let prayers be
given with thanke. let our prayers be for
the continuance of the blessings which we
gave, and let our acknowledgment of pre=
sent blessings, be an incouragement for fu=
ture. pray and praise togeather; pray
thankefully, pray not suspitiously. for be=
loued in the bowells of Christ Jesus, before
whose face I stand now, and before whose
face, I shall not be able to stand amongst the
righteous at the last day, if I ly now, and
make this pulpit my seat, to want
be christirate in the presence of you
a goly part (I hope) of the militant
church, ofwhich I am, in the presence of
ye whole triumphant church of which,
by grace, in whome I am that I am, I
hope to be, in the presence of the head of
that whole church which is all in all, I,
ends I thinke, that I gaue the spirit of
god, 1 Corinthians 7.40, it I am sure
I gaue

in that former place, apparrels a subiects 952

prayer well, when he says, let prayers be 953

giuen with thanks. let our prayers be for 954

the continnuance of the blessings which we 955

haue, and let our acknowledgment of pre= 956

sent blessings, be an inducement for fu= 957

ture. pray and prayse togeather; pray 958

thankefully, pray not suspitiously. for be= 959

loued in the bowells of Christ Iesus, before 960

whose face I stand now, and before whose 961

face, I shall not be able to stand amongst the 962

righteous, at the last day, if I ly now, and 963

make this ~~profit my~~ Pulpit my shop, to uent 964

Sophisticate wares, ~~wares~~ in the presence of you 965

a holy part (I hope) of the Militant 966

Church, of which I am, in the presence of 967

the whole triumphant Church of which, 968

by him, <u>in</u> whome I am that I am, I 969

hope to be, in the presence of the head of 970

* <u>that</u> whole Church who is all in all, I, 971

and I <u>thinke, that</u> I haue the spirit of 972

god, *1 Corinthians 40 7.40*, (I ~~hau~~ am sure I haue 973

---

969 by
971 the
972 *thinke*
973 [F50 has *1 Cor.7.44.* in margin]

I haue not testified it in m[any] g[rea]t point)e, and
I may be thought to know somethinge in
Ciuill affayres, (I am sure I haue not been
stupefied in these points) do deliuer that,
w[h]ich vpon the tryall of a Morall Man,
and a Christian Man, and a Devoute Man,
I beleeue to be true, that so weh is the
breath of our Nostrills, y[e]t, in g[rea]t dant, soe
far from submittinge it to that Idolatry,
and Superstition, that did heretofore oppresse
vs, as his immediate predecessor, whose
Memory is iustly pretious to you, was.
These wayes may be diuers, and yet both
end the same, the glorie of god. And to a
iuster comparison, then will you, I know
I cannot carry it.

This is the breath of our Nostrills, our breath,
is his, that is our Spheere. first in the con=
tayning it, not to speake in his diminution,
then in vttringe it amongst Men, to inter=
pret fayrely and loyally his proce=dinge and then in
vttring yt to god, in sure prayers, for his
        continuance

I haue not resisted it in this ~~house~~,) I, and   974

^point^

I may be <u>thought</u> to know something in   975

Ciuill affayres, (I am sure I haue not been   976

stupified in <u>these points</u>) do deliuer that,   977

which ~~also~~ vpon the truth of a Morall Man,   978

and a Christian Man, and a Church Man,   979

<u>I beleeue</u> to be true, That he who is the   980

breath of our Nostrills, ys, in his hart, as   981

far from submitting vs to that Idolatry,   982

and superstition, <u>that</u> did heretofore oppresse   983

vs, as his imediate predecessor, whose   984

Memory is iustly pretious to you, ~~was~~.   985

was

<u>There</u> ways may be diuers, and yet theyr   986

<u>ends the same,</u> The glorie of god. And to a   987

higher Comparison, then <u>with her,</u> <u>I know</u>   988

<u>I cannot</u> carry it.   989

<u>He is</u> the breath of our Nostrills, our breath   *Vita*   990

is his, That is our speech. first <u>in the</u> con=   991

tayning it, not to speake in his diminution,   992

then in vttringe it amongst Men, to inter=   993

dings   **in**

pret fayrely and loyally his procee= and then ~~the~~   994

vttring yt to god, in such prayers, for the   995

continuance

---

975   allowed
977   this point
980   beleeve
983   which
986   Their
987   end the same, that is,
988   to her
988–89   I know not how to
990   As then
990M   [not in F50]
991   in

to intimate hereof, ws imply a thankefull
acknowledgment of the present blessings
spirituall and temporall weire we enioy
now by him. to breake is speare, but breake
is life too, and so our life is gib. how
willingly gib subiects would giue their
life for him, I make no doubt, but yo
doubt not. this is argument inough, for
their propensnes, to giue their lifes for
gib honor, or for his possessions gib
children, that though not contra voluntatem,
yet prater voluntatem, without any de=
claration of gib pleasure by command, they
haue been as ready voluntarily as if a
presse had commanded them. but those
wayes weire gib weisedome hate reason
for procuring peace, haue kept of gib will giue
gib subiects would giue here lifes for him.
yet their lifes are gib, who is the breath of
their Nostrills, And therefore though they
do not leaue them for him, Let them lead
them for him; though they be not called to
dy

<u>continuance</u> thereof, as imply a thankefull   996

acknowledgment of the present blessings   997

spirituall and temporall which we enioy   998

now, by him. <u>So</u> breath is speech, but breath   999

is life too, and so our lyfe is his. how   1000

willingly his subiects would giue their   1001

lifes for him, I make no doubt, but he   1002

doubts not. This is argument inough for   1003

their <u>propensnes</u>, to giue their lyfes for   1004

his honor, or for the possessions of his   1005

Children, that though not *contra* <u>*voluntatem*</u>,   1006

yet *præter voluntatem*, without any De=   1007

claration of his <u>pleasure by</u> command, they   1008

haue been as ready voluntarily as if a   1009

presse had commanded them. but <u>those</u>   1010

ways which his wisedome hath chosen   1011

for <u>procuring</u> peace, haue kept of. much tryall of that, how willinglie   1012

his Subiects <u>would giue there</u> lyfes for him.   1013

yet their lyfes are his, who is the breath of   1014

their Nostrills; And therefore though they   1015

do not leaue them for him, let them lead   1016

them for him; though they be not calld to   1017
dy

---

996   continuing
999   So farre,
1004 propensenesse and readinesse
1006 *voluntatem*, not against his will
1008 will, or pleasure, by any
1010 these
1012 the procuring of . . . much occasion of triall
1013 would have given their

dy for ye synn, yet let them liue so, as it
may be for ye synn: liue peaceably, liue
honestly, liue industriously; all this is for synn:
for ye synn of ye people endanger the
Prince, as much as his own. When it shall
be required at your hands, dy for synn.
In ye meane tyme liue for synn; liue so,
as your liuinge do not kindle gods anger
against synn, and have a good confession, that
he is ye breath of your Nostrills, that your
lyfe is his.

As then ye breath of our Nostrills is expressed
by this word in his text, Ruach, Spiritus,   Gen. 2.
Spreche, and lyfe, so it is his. When ye breath   7.
of lyfe was first breathed into man, there
it is called by another word, Neshamah and
hath the Soule, the immortall Soule: and is the Anima
knig ye breath of lyfe; is ye ye Soule of
his Subiects so, as that theyr Souls are
his? So as that they must shine towards
men, in iuiust actions, or sinne towards
god

dy for ~~to~~ him, ~~yet~~ let them liue so, as <u>it</u>   1018

may be for ~~to~~ him. <u>liue peaceably, liue</u>   1019

<u>honestly, liue industriously; all this is</u> for him,   1020

for the Sins of the people endanger the   1021

Prince, as much as his own. when <u>it</u> shall   1022

be required at your <u>hands,</u> Dy for him.   1023

In the meane tyme liue for him; liue so,   1024

as your liuinge do not kindle gods anger   1025

against him, and <u>thats</u> a good <u>confession</u>, that   1026

he is the breath of your Nostrills, that your   1027

lyfe is his.   1028

As then the breath of our Nostrills is expressd   1029

by this word in this text, *Ruach, Spiritus,*   *Gen.2.*   1030
                                                        7.
Speeche, and lyfe, so it is his. when the breath   1031

of lyfe was first breathd into man, there   1032

it is calld by another word, *Neshamah* and   1033

<u>thats</u> the Soule, the imortall Soule: and is the *Anima*   1034
       that
*   king ~~the~~ <u>breath of</u> lyfe? is he the soule of   1035
        ^
his Subiects so, as that theyr Souls are   1036

his? so as that they must sinne towards   1037
         sinne
Men, <u>in</u> iniust actions, or ~~fine~~ towards   1038
        ^   god

1018	that
1019–20	to live *peaceably*, to live *honestly*, to live *industriously*, is to live
1022	that
1023	hand, then
1026	that is . . . Confession, and acknowledgement
1034	that is
1035	the breath of that
1038	in doing

ni ... for sakinge or dishonowringe ... him,
if ye will saue theem. If I had the honor of
to aske this question in his royall preseure
I know ye would be the first man, that would
say no; No; your Souls are not myne,
Sr. And as ye is a most perfit text Man
in the booke of god (and by the way I
should not vastily, fear his beeing a papist
that is a good text-man) I know ye ..
would rite Daniel, houge our god do..
not deliuer ỹb, yet know, O king that
we will not worshipp thy gods; I know ye
would rite Sanct Peter, we ought to obey
god rather then man; And ye would
rite Christ himselfe, fear not them (for
the Souls) that cannot hurt the Souls. ye
claimes not ~~the~~ your Souls Sr. The
Ruach here tis not Neshamah; —
your life is his, your Soule is not
his in that sense. but yet beloued, —
the se

Act:
5.29.

in ~~dis~~ forsaking <u>or</u> dishonoring ~~god~~ him,   1039

*   if <u>he</u> will haue them? If I had the honor ~~of~~   1040

to aske this question in his royall presence,   1041

I know he would be the first Man, that would   1042

say no; No; your Souls are not myne,   1043

so. And as he is a most perfit text Man   1044

in the booke of god (and by the way I   1045

should not easily fear his beeing a papist   1046

that is a good text man) I know he   1047

would cite *Daniel*, <u>though</u> our god do   1048

not deliuer vs, yet know, O king that   1049

we will not worshipp thy gods; <u>I</u> know he   1050

would cite *Saint Peter*, we ought to obey   1051

Act: *   god rather then men; And he would   1052

5.29.   cite Christ himselfe, fear not them (for   1053

the soule) that cannot hurt the soule. he   1054

claimes not ~~the~~ your Souls so. <u>Tis</u>   1055

Ruach here, <u>tis</u> not *Neshamah*;   1056

your life is his, your soule is not   1057

his in that sense. but yet, beloued,   1058
                                                                these

---

1039 *God,* in . . . and
1040 the King
1048 saying, *Though*
1050 And I
1055 It is
1056 it is

these two words are promiscuously used
in the Scripture; Ruach is often the
soule; Neshamah is often but the tem=
porall lyfe: and howe far, the one as well
as the other, is his kinge, that he must
answer for your Souls; So they are
his; for he is not a kinge of bodyes, but
of men a kinge of men; bodies and --
Souls: now a kinge of men onely, but of
Christian men: So your religion, and your
Souls are his; his; apperteyninge to
his care. And therefore thinge you owe
no obedience to any power under heauen,
to decline you from the true god, or the
true worship of that god, and the funda=
mentall thinges hereof, yet in those thinges
which are in their nature but circum=
stantiall, and may therefore accordinge to
time, and place, and persons, admitt
alterations, in those thinges, those they
be

these two words are promiscuously vsd   1059

in the <u>Scripture</u>; *Ruach* is often the   1060

soule; *Neshamah* is <u>often but</u> the tem=   1061

porall lyfe: and thus far, the one as well   1062

as the other, is the kings, That he must   1063

aunswer for your Souls; So they are   1064

his; for he is not a king of bodyes, but   1065

~~of Men~~ a king of Men; bodies and   1066

Souls; nor a king of Men onely, but of   1067

Christian men: so your religion, <u>and</u> your   1068

Souls are his; <u>his</u>; appertayning to   1069

his <u>care</u>. And therefore though you owe   1070

no obedience to any power vnder heauen,   1071

<u>to</u> decline you from the true god, or the   1072

true worship of that god, **in** ~~and~~ the funda= 1073

mentall things thereof, yet in those things   1074

which are in their nature but Circum=   1075

stantiall, and may therefore according to   1076

time ~~truth~~, <u>and place</u>, and persons, admitt 1077
^

* <u>alteration</u>s, in those things, though they 1078
                                          be

1060 Scriptures
1061 often
1068 so
1069 his, that is,
1070 *care, and his account*
1072 so as to
1073 and
1077 times, and places
1078 alterations

to bringe ~~repentaunnce~~ to religion, submitt your selfe to his direction, for heere hee two words meete, Ruach, and Neshamah your lifes are his gift, and your Souls are gift: his end being to advance godes truth, you are bound to trust him with his way. hee is Spiritus, as it is his tholie ghost, an instrument of his tholie ghost, to convey blessings to vs; Sⁱpiritus, as it is our breath, our spyrer; Spiritus, as it is our lyfe, Spiritus as it is our Soule, even in bringe concerninge his Soule, so far as temporall bringe concerne Spirituall, as tymes off meetings and proceedings when we are mett ~~for~~ he is his breath of our Nostrills, our spyrer, our life, our Soule, in that limited sense, are gift.

But did hese Subverte of his (and I reare none but his Subverte with hys plot.

be things ~~altering~~ to religion, submitt your   1079
appertaynynge

selfs to his <u>direction</u>, for here the two   1080

words meete, *Ruach,* and *Neshamah,*   1081

your lifes are <u>his his</u>, and your Souls   1082

are <u>his</u>: his end being to aduance gods   1083

truth, <u>you are bound to trust him with</u>   1084

the way. He is <u>*Spiritus, as it*</u> is the   1085

<u>Holie ghost, an instrument of the Holie</u>   1086

<u>ghost</u>, to convey blessings <u>to vs; *Spiri*</u>=   1087

<u>*tus, as it our breath, our*</u> speech;   1088

<u>*Spiritus,* as it is our lyfe, *Spiritus*</u>   1089

<u>as it is our Soule, Euen in things con</u>=   1090

<u>cerninge the Soule, so far as tem</u>=   1091

<u>porall things</u> concerne Spirituall, as   1092

tymes of <u>meetings and proceedings when we are mett,</u>   1093

~~for~~ he is the breath of our Nostrills,   1094

our speech, our <u>life</u>, our Souls, in that   1095

limited sense, are his.   1096

<u>But</u> did those Subiects of his (and I   1097

charg none but his Subiects with this   1098
plot

1080	directions
1082	his
1083	his too
1084	he is to be trusted much, in matters of *indifferent* nature, by
1085	the word of our Text, *Spiritus,* as *Spiritus*
1086–87	Holy Ghost, so farre, by accommodation, as that he is Gods instrument . . . upon us
1087–88	and as *spiritus* is our *breath,* or
1089–92	and as it is *our life,* and as it is *our soule* too, so farre, as that in those temporall things which
1093	meeting, and much of the *manner* of proceeding, when we are met) we are to receive directions from him:
1094	So
1095	*lives*
1097	But then,

plot) from whome god deliuered them his
day, did they thinke so oft them, that he
was the breath of our Nostrills? If the
breath be soure, if it be tainted and
corrupt (as they) would nedes thinke in
this case) is that good Philosophie, for
an yll breath, to cut of the head, to suff-
rate it to smother, to strangle, to
murder that man? Thes is the breath
of their Nostrills, they owe them their
prayer, their hearts, their prayers,
and then gaue these ... of folk
made them their songes, and they
byword? Thes gaue these drunkards
men ... of the Babilonian ...
made Libells against them? How gaue
these Seminatores verborum, de=
famed them with contrary defamations,
then, that he persecuted their religion,
when he did not, now that he ... lost
his

Job:
30.1

Act: 17.
18

plot) from whome god deliuerd <u>him</u> this   1099

day, did they thinke so of him, that he   1100

was the breath of our Nostrills? If the   1101

breath be soure, if it be tainted and   1102

corrupt, (as they would needs thinke in   1103

this case), is <u>that</u> good Phisicke, for   1104

an yll breath, to cut of the head, <u>to</u> suffo=   1105

cate it, to smother, to strangle, to   1106

murder that man? He is the breath   1107

of their Nostrills, they owe him theyr   1108

Speech, theyr thanks, theyr prayers,   1109

and how haue these Children of fools   1110

made him theyr Songe, and theyr   *Job:*   1111

by word? How haue these Drunkards,   *30.1*   1112

Men drunke <u>of</u> the *Babilonian* Cup   1113

made libells against him? How haue   1114

these <u>*Seminatores verborum*</u>; de=   1115

famd him, <u>with</u> contrary defamations,   *Act: 17.*   1116
                                                  18

<u>Then</u>, that he persecuted theyr religion,   1117

when he did not, now that he hath lefte   1118
              his

1099 plot, for, *I judge not them who are without . . .* us
1104 it
1105 or to
1113 with
1115 those *Seminatores verborum, word-scatterers*
1116 even with
1117 Heretofore

his owne religion when he eate not? Lo
it heir breade, they owe him their tongues,
and how fouly do they speake; theyr
breade, they owe him theyr life, and how
prodigally did they giue away theyr
liues, to take away his? Lo it theyr
breade, theyr Soule, that is accomptant
for theyr Soule, (though his account to
god will be easie for them) and how haue
they rased themselfe out of his Audit,
withdrawen themselfe from god Allegor=
ance. This they haue donne Historically:
and to say prophetically what they would
do, first theyr extenuation of his fact,
when they call it an enterprise of a
few unfortunate gentlemen, and then
theyr exaltation of his fact, when
they make a principall person in it,
a Martyr, his is prophecie enough, that
sure they are not ashamed of that ori=
ginall

his own <u>religion when he hath not</u>? He   1119

is their breath, they owe him their tongues,   1120

and how fouly do they speake; <u>theyr</u>   1121

<u>breath,</u> they owe him theyr lifs, and how   1122

prodigally <u>did</u> they giue away their   1123

<u>lifes, to</u> take away his? He is theyr   1124

<u>breath, their</u> Soule, that is accomptant   1125

<u>for their Souls, (though his account to</u>   1126

<u>god will be easie for them)</u> and how haue   1127

they <u>rasd</u> themselfs out of his Audit,   1128

<u>withdrawen</u> themselfs from his Allege=   1129

ance? This they haue donne Historically: 1130

and to say prophetically what they would   1131

do, first theyr extenuation of this fact,   1132

when they call it an enterprise of a   1133

few vnfortunate gentlemen, and then   1134

theyr exaltation of this fact, when   1135

they make a̬ principall person in it,   1136

a Martyr, this is prophecie enough, that   1137

since they are not ashamed of <u>that</u> Ori=   1138
                                              ginall

1119	Religion
1121–22	and
1123	do
1124	lives to others, that they might
1125	breath, (as breath is the
1126–27	*for their soules,*
1128	raised
1129	and withdrawne
1138	the

...miall, they will not be afraid to repeate
it often, and pursue the same practise
till they have their end.

Let it be Josiah, let it be Zedechiah, unctus
he was the breath of their nostrills, that   Domi=
was the first attribute, and he was the   ni.
anointed of the lord, that is the next.
So that it pleased allwayes separated that
were anointed from prophane..
and secular use. Unction was a re=
ligious distinction. It had that ministra=
tration in practise, before any law
given for it. When Jacob had had
that vision in sleeping upon his stone,
were made him see that that place
was the house of god and the gate
of heaven, then he tooke that stone, and   Gen:
set it up for a pillar, and anointed it.   28:18.
This was the practise in nature; and
then the precept in the law, was, as
                for

ginall, they will not be affraid to coppie 1139

it often, and pursue the same <u>practise</u> 1140

<u>till they haue their</u> end. 1141

let it be <u>*Iosiah*</u>, let it be *Zedechiah*,   *Vnctus* 1142

he was <u>the breath of his Subiects,</u> that   *Domi=* 1143
                                                       ni.

was the first attribute, and he was the 1144

anointed of the lord, <u>that is the next</u>: 1145

vnction it selfe allways seperated that 1146

which was anointed from prophane 1147

and secular vse: Vnction was a re= 1148

ligious distinction. It had that signi= 1149

fication in practise, before any law 1150

<u>giuen</u> for it. When *Jacob* had had 1151

that **vision** ~ <u>sleeping vpon his</u> stone, 1152

which made him see that that place 1153

was the house of god and the gate 1154
                             that
of heauen, then he <u>tooke</u> ~~that~~ <u>stone</u>, and   *Gen:* 1155
                                                  28.18.

set it vp for a pillar, and anointed it. 1156

This was the practise in nature; and 1157

then the precept in the law, was, as 1158
                          for

1140 practises
1141 to the same
1142 *Iosiah* then
1143 the Breath, the life of his Subjects, {and
1145 which is the other
1151 was given
1153 upon the
1155 tooke up that stone which he had stept upon

for the altar it selfe, & for many other
thinges belonginge to the service of god, in
the temple, thou shalt anoint them, to
Exo:
29.36.
sanctifie them. Thus it was for thinges,
and then if we touche persons, we
see the dignitie that anointinge gaue, for
it was giuen but to three sorts of per=
sons, to kinges, to priests, and to
Prophets: Kinges, and Priests had it to
testifie their ordinarie and permanent
and indelible iurisdiction: Their power is
layd on in oyle; and prophets had it because
they were extraordinarily raysed to de=
1 reg:
19.15.
nounce and to execute gods iudgments
vpon persons that were anointed, vpon
Priests and Kinges too, in these cases:
for there they were particularly em=
ployd. Thus then it is, Anointed thinges
could not be touchd but by anointed
persons; and their anointed persons
could not be touchd but by persons
anointed;

for the altar it selfe, so for many other   1159

things belonging to the service of god, in   1160

Exo: the temple, Thou shalt anoint them, to   1161
29.36.
              sanctifie them. Thus it was for things,   1162

and then if we consider persons, we   1163

see the dignitie that anointing gaue, for   1164

it was giuen but to three sorts of per=   1165

sons, To *Kings*, to *Preists*, and to   1166

Prophets. Kings, and Preists had it to   1167

testifie their ordinarie and permanent   1168

and indelible iurisdiction: Theyr power is   1169

layd on in Oyle; and prophets had it, because   1170

1 reg: they were extraordinarily raysd to de=   1171

19.15.   nounce and to execute gods iudgments   1172

vpon persons that were anointed, vpon   1173

Preists <u>and</u> kings too, in those cases,   1174

for which they <u>were</u> particularly em=   1175

ployd. Thus then it is, Anointed things   1176

could not be touchd but by anointed   1177

persons; and then anointed persons   1178

could not be touchd but by persons   1179
                          anointed;

1171–72M [not in F50]
1174   and upon
1175   were then

28

anointed; the priest not ~~anointed~~ directed but by
the king, the king, as king, not corrected
but by the prophet. And this was the
state that they lamented so compassio=
nately, that their king, thus anointed, --
thus recompted, was taken prisoner
saw his sonne slaine in his presence
then had his owne eyes pulled out and was
bound in chaines, and carried to Babel.
And least that this, in himselfe, and in his
sonne, and in all, was not intended, they
say, against our, not Zedechiah but
Josias; for doubt (speaking in nature)
gave all particular misteryes in it. An
anointed king (and many kings anointed
here are not) and so that he (unctus
prae Consortibus, above his fellow kings,
for, I thinke no other king of his religion,
is anointed) the anointed of the Lord,
he who in his text gave both these great
names

directed
anointed; The preist not ~~derected~~ but by 1180
                     ^

*   the king, The king, as king, not corrected 1181

but by the prophet. And this was the 1182

state that they lamented so compassio= 1183

natly, that theyr king, thus anointed, 1184

thus exempted, was taken prisoner, 1185

saw his <u>Sonne</u> slaine in his presence, 1186

                    and
<u>then had his own eys pulld out</u>, was 1187
                    ^

bound in chaines, and carried to *Babel*. 1188

And lesse then this, in himselfe, and in his 1189

sonne, and in all, was not intended, this 1190

day, against our, not *Zedechiah* but 1191

Josias; for death (speaking in nature) 1192

hath all particular miseryes in it. An 1193

anointed king (and many kings anointed 1194

there are not) and he that is <u>*vnctus*</u> 1195

præ <u>*consortibus*</u>, aboue his fellow kings, 1196

(for, I thinke no other king of his religion, 1197

is anointed) The anointed of the lord, 1198

<u>he who</u> in this Text hath both <u>these</u> great 1199
                          names

1186 Sonnes
1187 and then had his owne eyes pulled out
1195 anoynted
1196 *Consortibus suis*
1199 who . . . those

named Meshiach Jehouah, christus
Domini, as though he had been but the humi=
ble anointed for king of the Iewes, and so
made the fitter fuell for their fire, as
though, (as Dauids lamentation is for
Saul) he had not been anointed with
oyle, The vij. of god, he by whome god
looke vpon vs, The hand of god, he by
whome god protects vs, The powre of god,
by whome in his due tyme, (and Vsque
quo Domine how long o lord before that
tyme come?) god shall tread downe his
owne and our enemies, that swallowd
and deuourd by them, in their infallible
assurance of his reuenge. So it was
historically. And how it stands prophe=
tically, that is what sure, as they were,
would do for the future, as long as
they write, not in libells clandestinely and
surreptitiously stolln out, but with publiq
publique autority, That our thoughts are

Iudg:
9. 8.

2. Sam:
1. 21.

Coguere
teeth

110

names *Meshiach Jehouah, Christus* 1200

Domini, As though he had been but the bram= 1201

Iudg:
9.8.

ble anointed for king of the trees, and so 1202

made the fitter fuell for their fire, As 1203

though, (as *Dauids* lamentation is for 1204

Saul) he had not been anointed with 1205

2. Sam:
1.21.

oyle, This ey of god, He by whome god 1206

looks vpon vs, This hand of god, He by 1207

whome god protects vs, This foote of god, 1208

<u>by</u> whome, in his due tyme, (and *vsque* 1209

quo Domine how long o lord before that 1210

tyme come?) god shall tread downe his 1211

own and our enemies, was swallowd -- 1212

and deuourd by them, in <u>theyr</u> infallible 1213

assurance of his perishinge. So it was 1214

Historically. And how it stands prophe= 1215

tically, that is what such as they ~~are~~ were 1216

would do for the future, As longe as 1217

* ~~Coquaeus~~
~~fo. 18~~

they write, not in libells clandestinely and 1218

subreptitiously stolln out, but <u>with</u> ~~publiq~~ 1219

publique autority, That our Preists are 1220
no

1209   he by
1213   their confidence of their owne plot, and their
1218M Coquaeus.*fo.*18
1219   avowed by

no anointed priests, but the priests of
Baal, for that they write, that the con=
spiracy of his day being against him,
who oppressed religion, was as ill, as
that against Josias, who did not *but* oppresse 39.
his state and that they write, that 43.
these who were the actors, and heretofore
said, because at their execution they
submitted all to the Romane Church, and
and were content, if that Church con=
demned it true, then to repent it, so 78.
they write to. That the religion of our
present king, is no better then the reli=
gion of Jeroboam, or of Numa Pom=
pilius, because they write, that the
last Queene being an heretique, yet 65.
because she was anointed did cure
the disease, the kings evill, but be=
cause in ... he the king refused
to be anointed at his Coronation, there=
fore he could cure that disease, and
therefore

no anointed <u>preists</u>, but the priests of 1221

Baal, for <u>that</u> they write; <u>That</u> the Con= 1222

spiracy of this day beeing against him, 1223

who oppressd religion, was as iust, as 1224

that against *Cæsar*, who did <s>not</s> ^but^ op03sse   <u>39</u>. 1225

the state, and <s>they</s> that they write; That 1226

    <u>43</u>.

those who were the <u>actors</u>, are therefore 1227

saud, because at theyr execution they 1228

submitted all to the Romane Church, 1229

and were content, if <u>that</u> Church con= 1230

*   demnd <u>that fact, then to repent yt,</u> so   <u>78</u>. 1231

they write <u>to</u>; That the religion of our 1232

present king, is no better then the reli= 1233

gion of *Jeroboam*, or of *Numa Pom=* 1234

pilius, <u>that also they write</u>; That the 1235

last *Queene* though an Heretique, yet   <u>65</u>. 1236

because she was Anointed did cure 1237

that disease, The kings evyll, but be= 1238

cause in scorne thereof the king refusd 1239

to be anointed at his Coronation, there= 1240

fore he cannot cure that disease, and 1241
          therefore

1221   *no Priests*
1222   *so . . . Thai*
1225M *fol. 39.*
1227   *actors herein*
1227M *fol. 43.*
1230   *the*
1231   *it, then to repent the Fact, for*
1231M *fol. 78.*
1232   *also*
1235   *for so they write too*
1236M *fol. 65.*

~~therefore~~ Non dicendus sanctus domini sayth that autor, (for all those are the words of one Man, and one who had no other occasion to say all this, but onely) the kings Apology for the oath of Allegiance) by retayning and relyinge upon sure autors and autorities as those, were remayne for theyr future instruction, we see theyr disposition for the future, and iudge of them prophetically, as well as Historically).

Now the misery which is here lamented, the declination of the kingdome in the person of the king, is here very fulle, she was taken in theyr pitty. Taken taken in pitty, taken in theyr pitty, are so many stayings downe, so many decrease, so many gradations or rather degradations in this calamity. Let it be Josiah, let it be Zedechiah, they were taken, taken and never restored.

Let

Captus.

                      i

therefore <u>*Non d̶u̶cendus vnctus Domini*</u>,   1242

says that autor, (for all these are the   1243

words of one Man; and one who had no   1244

other <u>occasion</u> to say all this, but onely   1245

the kings Apology for the Oath of Alle=   1246

geance,) by <u>retayning and</u> relyenge   1247

vpon such autors, and autorities as <u>those</u>,   1248

which remayne for theyr future in=   1249

struction, we see theyr <u>disposition</u> for   1250

the future, and iudge of them propheti=   1251

cally as well as historically.   1252

    Now the misery which is here lamented,   1253

Captus. the declination of the kingdome in the   1254

person of the king, is thus expressd,   1255

He was taken in theyr pitts. <u>Taken,</u>   1256

<u>Taken in pitts,</u> Taken in their pitts, are   1257

so many <u>stayres downe</u>, so many des=   1258

cents, so many gradations o̶r̶ rather   1259

degradations in this calamity. let it   1260

be *Josiah*, let it be *Zedechiah*, they   1261

* were taken, taken and neuer <u>rescued</u>.   1262
                                let

1242	so *non dicendus unctus Domini*, he is not to be called the Anointed of the Lord
1245	provocation
1247	retaining in their avowed books, and by
1248	these
1250	dispositions
1256–57	*taken*, and taken in *pits*, and
1258	staires
1262	returned

Let it be our Iosiah, and will it hold
in that application? was he taken?
He was plotted for; but was he taken? when he himselfe takes knowledge, he
that both at home and abroade, those of
the Romane perswasion, assurd them=
selfe of some especiall worke, for
the aduancement of theyr cause at
that tyme, when they had taken that
assurance, he was taken, taken in
theyr assurance, infallibly taken in
theyr opinion. As theyr kingdome
was taken in theyr opinion, who thought
that Navy invincible, so this king was
taken in theyr assurance, who thought
that plot infallible.
He was taken. And in foueis, in pitts sayd Eouen
he lept. If our first translation would
serue, the sorrow were the lesse, for there
it is, he was taken in theyr Net; now, a
now that flatterers spreadeth a Net;

let it be our *Josiah*, and will it hold 1263

in that application? was he taken? 1264

He was plotted for; but was he ta= 1265

ken? when he himselfe <u>takes</u> knowledge, ~~*Jos.*~~ 1266
~~*49.*~~

That both at home and abroade, those of 1267

the Romane persuasion, assurd them= 1268

selfs of some especiall worke, for 1269

the aduancement of theyr cause at 1270

that tyme, when they had taken that 1271

assurance, he was <u>taken</u>, taken in 1272

<u>their</u> assurance, infallibly taken in 1273

theyr opinion. <u>As</u> this kingdome 1274

was taken in theyr opinion, who thought 1275

<u>that</u> Nauy inuincible, so this king was 1276

taken in theyr assurance, who thought 1277

<u>that</u> plot infallible. 1278

He was taken, And <u>in *foueis*, in pitts</u>, says *Fouea* 1279

the text. If our first translation would 1280

serve, the sorrow were the lesse, for there 1281

it is, He was taken in theyr Net; now, a 1282

man that flattereth spreadeth a Net; 1283
a

1266 takes publique
1272 so taken
1273 that their
1274 so, as
1276 their
1278 this
1279 *in fovea, in a pit*

pro:29.
5.

Examine that differems not a flatterer from
a Counsaylor, is taken in a net: but
that not so desperate as in a pit. In
Josiahs case it was a pit, a Snare
it was as was spoken. In our Josiahs case
in Zedechiahs case it was fully as it

Foucis

is in the text, not in Fouea, but in
foueis, plurally, in their pitts, in their
diuers pitts; doeth in the Mynd, doeth in
the Coller.

illorum

And then it was in Foucis illorum, sayd
the text, in their pitts but the text does not
tell vs in whose. In the verse before,
it is sayd our persecutors did this, and
this, And then it followes he was taken in
their pitts; in the persecutors pitt certainely, but yet who are they? If it
were Josiah, the persecutor was Necho

2 Chro:
35. 23.

King of Egypt, for from his army Josiah
receyued his deaths wound; If it were
Zedechiah, the persecutor he was
Nebuchadnezzar, king of Babilon,
for he carried Zedechiah into Cap-
tivity)

<u>Prince</u> that discerns not a flatterer from   1284

pro: 29.
5.
a Counsaylor, is taken in a net: but   1285

thats not so desperate, as in a pit. In   1286

Josiahs case it was a pit, a Graue,   1287
it was a pit a prison In our *Josiahs* case
*
In Zedechiahs case ʌ it was fully as it   1288

*Foueis
is in the Text, Not in *fouea*, but in   1289

foueis, plurally in their pits, In their   1290

diuers pits; <u>Death in the Myne, Death in</u>   1291

<u>the Cellar.</u>   1292

Illorum
And then it was in *Foueis illorum*; <u>says</u>   1293

<u>the Text, in theyr pits</u>, but the text does not   1294

tell vs in whose. In the verse before,   1295

it is said our persecutors did this, and   1296

this, <u>And then</u> it follows he was taken in   1297

their pits; in the persecutors <u>pitt</u> cer=   1298

tainely; but yet who are they? If it   1299

were <u>*Iosiah*</u>, the persecutor was *Necho*   1300

2 Chro:
king of Egipt, for from his army *Iosiah*   1301

35.23.
receyud his deaths wound; If it were   1302

Zedechiah, the persecutor ~~the~~ was   1303

Nebuchadnezzar, king of *Babilon*,   1304

for he carried *Zedechiah* into Cap=   1305
tiuity

1284   and a Prince
1285M   [not in F50]
1291–92 death in the mine where they beganne, death in the Cellar where they pursued their
            mischiefe
1293–94 in *their pits*, says the Text
1297   then
1298   pits
1300   *Iosiah* that was taken

trinity: Certenly the Holy ghost knew well inough, and could have spoke playne, whose these pitts were, but it pleasd him to forbeare Names. Certaynely our Josiah knowes well inough, whose these pitts, that were digged for him, were; but according to his naturall sweetnes, to decline the drawing of more blood, then necessarily he must, or his layenge of imputations and aspersions upon more then necessarily he must, he hath forborne Names. The Holy ghost knowes better then all the expositors in all our Libraries, who digged these pitts; our Josiah knowes better then all we who come but to Solemnize his deliverance, whose hands, and whose counsayles were in the digging of these pitts too.

He was taken, sayth our text. Trye it in First Josiah, who was taken, and never taken back, Trye it in Zedechiah who was

tiuity: Certenly the Holy ghost knew well 1306

inough, and could haue <u>spoke</u> playne, whose 1307

these pitts were; but it pleasd him to for= 1308

bear Names. Certaynely our *Josiah* 1309

knowes well inough, whose those pitts, <u>that</u> 1310

were digged for him, were; but according 1311

to his naturall sweetnes, to decline the 1312

drawing of more blood, then necessarily he 1313

must, or the layenge of imputations and 1314

aspersions vpon more then necessarily he 1315

must, he hath forborne Names. The Holy 1316

ghost knowes better then all the expositors 1317

in all our libraries, who diggd those pitts; 1318

Our *Josiah* knows better then all we who 1319

come but to <u>Solemnize</u> the deliuerance, 1320

whose hands, and whose counsayls were in 1321

the digging of these pitts too. 1322

He was taken, <u>says our Text</u>. fixe <u>it</u> in   *Fuit* 1323

Josiah, who was taken, and neuer ta= 1324

ken back, fixe it in *Zedechiah* who 1325
          was

1307   spoken
1310   which
1320   celebrate, and solemnize
1323   says our Text: *fuit*, hee *Was . . . that*
1323M [not in F50]

was taken, and never taken back, they both
perished, in both them here is iust cause of
perpetuall and permanent lamentation;
But transferr it to our Josiah, and then
he was taken, yet, he was but taken;
God did not suffer his holy one to see cor=
ruption; and so his lamentation is changed
to a congratulation: So our HA is an
Euge, our exclamation turned to acclam-
ation, so our De profundis, is a Gloria
in Excelsis, the pit the vault, is become
a hill, when we behold the power of
our great God; the Sepher kinoth, the
booke of lamentation is become Sepher Te-
hillim ~ ~ the booke of psalms, and thanke
givinge; Davids bonus es omnibus,
o Lord thou art good to all, yet come to
Moses his Non taliter omni; Thou
hast not dealt so well with any Nation, as
with us; And when we might have feard
a Dereliquisti, that god hath forsaken
us

was taken, and neuer taken back, they both 1326

perishd, in both them there is iust cause of 1327

perpetuall and permanent <u>lamentation</u>; 1328

But transfer it to our *Josiah*, and then 1329

He was taken, ys, He was but taken; 1330

God did not suffer his holy one to see <u>cor</u>= 1331

<u>ruption</u>; and so the lamentation is <u>changd</u> 1332

<u>to</u> a congratulation: so our *Væ* is an 1333

Euge, our exclamation turnd to accla= 1334

mation, <u>so</u> our *De profundis*, is a *Gloria* 1335

in *Excelsis*, the pit the vault, is become 1336

a hill, <u>when as</u> <u>we</u> behold the power of 1337
^ce^

our great god; <u>The</u> Sepher *kinoth*, The 1338

booke of <u>lamentation</u>, is become **Sepher Te**= 1339

hillim ~~. The booke of **psalms**, and <u>thanks</u> 1340
psalms ^

<u>giuinge</u>; *Dauids bonus es omnibus*, 1341

<u>O lord</u> thou art good to all, ys come to 1342

Moses his Non taliter omni, Thou 1343

hast not <u>dealt</u> so well with any Nation, as 1344

with vs; <u>And</u> when we might haue feard 1345

a *Derelinquisti*, that god had forsaken 1346
vs

1328   lamentation, and no roome left, for the exercise of any other affection
1331–32   *Correction*, nor God did not suffer his Anointed, to perish in this taking
1332–33   become (as wee said at first)
1335   and so
1337   from whence we may
1338   this
1339   Lamentations
1340–41   thanksgivings
1341   And *Davids*
1342   *Lord*
1343   *Moses non taliter, Lord*
1344   *done*
1345   for

vs, we had Saint Augustines Appropin=
quavi et nesciebam, we came nearer
and nearer to god, and knew yt not; we
knew not our danger, and therefore knew
not his especiall protection. Yt was one
particular degree of his Mercy, to proceed
so: as it is an ease to a Man not to know
of his friends sicknes, till he know it by..
warning of his recovery; so god did not
shew vs, with ye danger, till he established
vs with ye deliverance. and by making
his Servant and our Soueraigne, ye
blessed meanes of ye discovery; and ye
deliveraunce, he hath directed vs in all
apprehensions of daungers, to rely vpon
that wisedome in Ciuil affaires of state,
and vpon that zeale in causes of religion,
which he hath imprinted in his Royall
soule; historically god hath donne great
things for vs, by him; prophetically god
hath great things to do for vs, and all
ye

32

vs, we had _Saint Augustins_ Appropin=   1347

quaui _et_ nesciebam, we came nearer   1348

<u>and</u> nearer to god, and knew yt not; we   1349

*   **we**
<u>know</u> not our danger, and <u>therefore knew</u>   1350
                               ^

not his <u>espetiall</u> protection. It was one   1351

particular degree of his Mercy, to proceed   1352

so: as it is an ease to a Man not to hear   1353

of his frinds sicknes, till he hear it by   1354

hearing of his recouery, so god did not   1355

shake vs <u>with</u> the danger, till he establishd   1356

vs with the deliuerance. and by making   1357

his Seruant and our Soueraigne, the   1358

blessed meanes of <u>the</u> discouery, and <u>the</u>   1359

deliuerance, he hath directed vs in all   1360

apprehensions of dangers, to rely vpon   1361

that Wisedome in <u>Ciuil</u> affaires of state,   1362

and vpon that zeale, in causes of religion,   1363

which he hath imprinted in <u>his Royall</u>   1364

Soule; Historically god hath donne great   1365

things for vs, by him, prophetically god   1366

hath great things to do for vs, and all   1367
                               the

1347 S. *August.*
1348 &
1349 &
1350 knew . . . therefore knew
1351 special
1356 with the knowledge of
1359 that . . . that
1362 civill affaires,
1364 that

the Christian world, and will make him the
gods instrument to do them:

Auxiliaries we reserved at first, for the last gaspe, for
the knott to try of all, this consideration
that he who was truly affected with the said
hurtfull sure a danger, and the present sense
of such a deliueraunce, would also use all
meanes to his power, to secure the future,
That the kingdome in that king might
allwayes be safe from the like dangers:
No doubt our Josiah does that, in that were
appertayned vnto him; and all (the rest
of all) appertanies vnto him. If god had
made him his made to strange chords with
warrs and armies, we might be afraid,
that when god had donne his worke by
him, he would cast the redd into the fire:
god does not allwayes blesse these instru=
ments who loue blood, though he y pre=
tend his glorie: but since god hath
made him his doue, to fly ouer the
world with the Oliue braunc, with en=
deuours of peare in all places, as the
                                        Doue

	the Christian world, and will make him ~~the~~	1368
	his instrument to do them.	1369
Auxilia.	<u>We</u> reserud at first, for the last gaspe, <u>for</u>	1370
	the knott to ty vp all, this consideration,	1371
	That he <u>who</u> was truly affected <u>with</u> the sad	1372
	sense of such a danger, and the pious sense	1373
	of such a deliuerance, would also vse all	1374
	means <u>to</u> his power, to secure the future,	1375
	That <u>the</u> kingdome in that king might	1376
*	allways be safe from the like dangers..	1377
	No doubt, our *Josiah* <u>does</u> that, in that which	1378
	<u>appertaynes</u> vnto him; <u>and all</u> (the care	1379
	of all) <u>appertaines</u> vnto him. If god had	1380
	made him his rodd to scourge others with	1381
	warrs and armies, we might be afraid,	1382
	that when god had donne his worke by	1383
	him, he would cast the rodd <u>into</u> the fire:	1384
	god <u>does</u> not allways blesse those instru=	1385
	ments who loue blood, though they pre=	1386
	tend his glorie: but since god hath	1387
	made him his Doue, to fly ouer the	1388
	world with the Oliue branch, with en=	1389
	deuours of peace in all places, as the	1390
	Doue	

1370 Now, we . . . and for
1372 that . . . in
1375 in
1376 that
1378 doth
1379 appertaineth . . . and *all*, that is,
1380 appertaineth
1384 *in*
1385 doth

...our ded, to shall your bring his aliue
branch to the Arke, endeuour onely, surely,
peace as may aduance the Glury of god,
and establish peace of Conscience in him
selfe.

The rest on his part, I shall pre serue
him; and for his preseruation, and ours
in him, these things are to be done on our
part. first, let Iob returne to god, so as
god may looke vpon his cloathes in the
righteousnes of Christ; who will not be
put on, as a fair gowne to couer your
cloathes; but first put off your Synns,
and then put on him; Synns of the tyme,
Sinns of your age, Sinns of your Sinns
of your complexion, Sinns of your pro=
fession; put of all; for, your time, your
             your Sinns
age, your complexion, and your pro=
fession shall not be damned, but you;
your selfe. Do not thinke that your
                      our
Sondays zeale, a weeke, can burne
out all your extortions, and oppressions,
and vsury, and bribery, and Simony,
                                    and

Ne
necce=
mus.

Doue did, <u>he</u> shall euer bring his oliue 1391

branch to the Arke, <u>endeuour</u> onely such 1392

peace as may aduance the Church of god, 1393

and establish peace of Conscience in him 1394

selfe. 1395

That care on his part, shall preserve   *Ne* 1396

him, and for his preservation, and ours   *pecce=* 1397
   mus.

in him, these things are to be donn on our 1398

part. first, let vs returne to god, so as 1399

god may looke vpon vs cloathd in the 1400

<u>righteousnes</u> of Christ; who will not be 1401

put on, as a fair gowne to couer course 1402

cloathes; but first put of your Synns, 1403

and then put on him; Syns of the tyme, 1404

sins of your age, sins of your Sex, sins 1405

of your Complexion, sins of your pro= 1406

fession; put of all; for, your time, your 1407

            your Sex
<u>age, your Complexion, and</u> your pro= 1408
              ^

fession shall not be damnd, but you; 1409

<u>your selfes.</u> Do not thinke that your 1410

       once
Sondays zeale, ~~nor~~ a weeke, can burne 1411
      ^

out all your extortions, and oppressions, 1412

and vsury, and <u>bribery</u>, and Simony, 1413
               and

1391   so he
1392   that is, endevour
1401   righteousnessc
1408   Age, your Sex, your Complexion,
1410   you your selves shall
1413   butchery

and remembrings, and wantonnes practises
from Monday, to Saterday). Do hy not hynke it
to be so with the spirituall Man, as with the
Naturall; in the naturall body), a great proportion of Choler will rectifie a p cold, or
old, or flegmatique man; So it well by
hauing so many roses, but a vehement Zeale
on Sonday does not rectifie the sick dayes
Sinner. To try out then, I am bound for want
of an afternoones Sermon, and to fast all
the weeke longe so, as neuer to tast good
sweete the Lord is, in blessing the East,
and withdrawinge the East from sin, this
is no good diet not onely, upon your allegeance to God, but upon your allegeance to the
King, be good. No prince can gaue a better guard the Subiects truly religious.

Quantus murus patria, is Saint Ambrose
          vir iustus
his holy declamation. The sins of former
tymes, the sins and prouocations of Ma-
nasseth lay heauy upon Iosiah, as well
as god loued him. The sins of our dayes
our sins, may open any prince to gods
                 anger

margin: 2 reg: 23. 26.

and chamberinge, and wantonnes practisd   1414

from Monday to Saterday. Do ~~th~~ not thinke it   1415

to be so with the spirituall Man, as with the   1416

Naturall; in <u>the</u> naturall body, a great pro=   1417

portion of Choler will rectifie a cold, or   1418

*   old, or flegmatique man; he is <u>well by</u>   1419

hauing so much <u>color</u>. but a vehement zeale   1420

on Sonday doth not rectifie the six dayes   1421

Sinner. To cry out then, I am sterud for want   1422

of an <u>afternoones</u> Sermon, and to fast all   1423

the weeke longe so, as neuer to tast how   1424

sweete the lord is, <u>in</u> Clensing thy hart,   1425

and withdrawinge thy hand from sin, this   1426

is no good diet. not onely vpon your allege=   1427

ance to god, but vpon your allegeance to the   1428

king, be good. No prince can haue a bet=   1429

ter guard then Subiects truly religious.   1430

vir iustus
Quantus murus patriæ, <u>is *Saint*</u> Ambrose   1431
                    ^

his holy <u>exclamation.</u> The sins of former   1432

2   tymes, the sins and prouocations of <u>*Ma*=</u>   1433
*reg:*23.
26.   <u>*nasseth*</u> lay heauy vpon *Josiah,* as well   1434

as god loud him. The sins of our days,   1435

our sins, may open any prince to gods   1436
                    anger

34

anger. This is the first way of preservinge
our Josiah, to turne away the wrate of god,
by our repentance of former, and abstinence
from future sin.

A second is to uphold his honor and estimation
with other men; especially amongst strangers
that live with us, who, for the most part value
value princes so, as they finde their sub=
iect to value them. Ambassadors have ever
been sacred persons, and partakers of great
priviledges. A prince that lives, as ours, in
the eye of many Ambassadors, is not, as the
children of Israel, in the midst of Cananites,
and Jebusites, and Amorites, who all watred
their destruction, but he is in the midst of
Tutelare Angells, Nationall Angells, who
study, by good grace, the peace and wellfare
of the Christian state. But all strangers in
the land are not noble, and candid, and in=
genuous Ambassadors; and even they
who are so
may be misled to an undervalue of the
prince, by rumors, by disloyall, and neg=
ligent spreche from the subiect. we have
not

anger. This is the first way of preservinge   1437

our *Josiah*, to turne away the wrath of god,   1438

by <u>our repentance of former, and abstinence</u>   1439

<u>from future sins</u>.   1440

A second is to vphold his honor and estimation   1441

with other men; espetially amongst strangers   1442

that liue with vs; who, for the most part ~~vale~~   1443

value princes so, as they find theyr Sub=   1444

iects to value them. Ambassadors haue euer   1445

been sacred persons, and partakers of great   1446

priuileges. A prince that lives, as ours, in   1447

*   the **Ey** of many Ambassadors, **is not**, as the   1448

Children of *Israel*, in the midst of Cananites,   1449

and *Jebusits*, and *Amonits*, who all watchd   1450

*   <u>their destruction</u>; but he is in the midst of   1451

Tutelar Angells, Nationall Angells, who   1452

study, by gods grace, <u>the peace</u> and well fare   1453

of the Christian state. <u>But</u> all strangers in   1454

*   the land are not noble, and can**d**id, and in=   1455

who are so

genuous Ambassadors; <u>and even they</u> ^   1456

may be misled to an vnderualue of the   1457

prince, by rumors, <u>by disloyall, and</u> neg=   1458

ligent speeches from the subiect. we haue   1459

not

1439–40   our abstinence from future sinnes, after our repentance of former
1441M   *Honor.*
1451   the destruction of *Israel*
1453   & as it becomes us to hope) the peace
1454   But then
1456   & even *Ambassadors* themselves
1458   and by disloyal; and by

not felt Salomons whipes, but our repininges,
and repininges, and discontents may bringe us
to Rehoboams Scorpions 1. reg: 12.11. This
way carr a part in his kinges safety, and
in our safety, to holo in our selfe, to convay to
strangers, a good estimation of that happy
gouerment, which is truly good in it selfe.

Subsidia: And then a third and more important way
towards his preservation, is a chearfull disposition to supplie, and to support, and to assist
him, with such thinges as are necessary for his
outward dignity. when god himselfe was
the immediate king of the Jsraelites and
gouernd them by himselfe, he tooke it yll,
that they would depart from him, who neer
ded nothing of theyrs; for there could be no
other king but must necessarily be supplied
from them. And yet whatsoever beloued, what
god, who needed nothing tooke. The sacri-
fices of the bowe, were sure, as would have
kept divers royall houses. Take a bill of
them

not felt *Salomons* whips, but our whinings,   1460

and repinings, and discontents may bringe vs   1461

to *Rehoboams* Scorpions <u>*i.reg: 12.11*</u>. This   1462

way hath a part in the kings safety, and   1463

in our safety, to hold in our selfs, <u>to</u> conuay to   1464

strangers, a good estimation of that happy   1465

gouerment, which is truly good in it selfe.   1466

Subsi=   And then a third, and verie important way   1467
dia

towards his preseruation, is a chearfull dis=   1468

position to supplie, and to support, and to assist   1469

him, with such things as are necessary for his   1470

outward dignity. when god himselfe was   1471

the immediate king of the *Israelits* and   1472

gouernd them by himselfe, he tooke it yll,   1473

that they would depart from him, who nee=   1474

ded nothing of theyrs; for there could be no   1475

other king but must necessarily be supplied   1476

<u>from</u> them. And yet, consider, beloued, what   1477

god, who needed nothing tooke. The sacri=   1478

fices of the Iews, were such, as would haue   1479

kept diuers royall houses. Take a byll of   1480
                                            them

1460 not yet
1462 [in F50's margin]
1464 and to
1477 by

2 Chro:
35.

them: But in one passeouer, that Iosiah kept,
and compare that and other the like with
the smallnes of the land, wherin they posses=
sed, and that that they gaue was a very ve=
ry great proportion. Now it is the ser=
uice of god to contribute to the king as
well as to the preist; he that giues to a
preist, shall haue a preists reward, he
that giues to the king shall haue a kings
reward, wherfore, in those cases, wheare to
giue to the king is to giue to god, wheare
the peace of the state, and the glory of
the gospell so much depends vpon the
sustentation of the outward honor and
splendor of the king. preserue him so,
and so shall he lesse be subiect to those
dangers.

But lastly, and especially, let vs preserue Religio
him, by preseruing god amongst vs in the
true and sincere profession of his religion.
Let not a mis-grounded and a disloyall
imagination, of coolnes in him, coole you
                                            in

them but in one passeouer, that *Josiah* kept,	*2 Chro:*	1481
and compare that, and other the like with	*35.*	1482
the smallnes of the land, <u>which</u> they posses=		1483
sed, <u>and that</u> that they gaue was a <u>very, ve=</u>		1484
<u>ry</u> great proportion. Now it is the ser=		1485
vice of god to contribute to the king as		1486
well as to the preist; He that giues to a		1487
prophet, shall haue a prophets reward, he		1488
that giues to the king shall haue a kings		1489
reward, a Crown, in those cases, where to		1490
giue to <u>the</u> king is to giue to god, <u>where</u>		1491
the peace of the state, and the glory of		1492
<u>the ghospell so much depends</u> vpon the		1493
sustentation of the <u>outward honor</u> and		1494
splendor of the king. preserve him so,		1495
and he shall the lesse be subiect to <u>those</u>		1496
<u>dangers.</u>		1497
But lastly, and espetially let vs preserve	*Religio*	1498
him, by preserving god amongst vs in the		1499
true and sincere profession of <u>his</u> religion.		1500
let not a mis-grounded <u>and a</u> disloyall		1501
imagination, of coolenes in him, coole you		1502

in

1483	that
1484	and you will see, that
1484–85	very
1491	your . . . that is, where
1493	God in his Gospel depends much
1494	estimation, and outward honour
1496–97	these dangers, of such falling into their pits
1500	our
1501	and

in your own families. Omnis spiritus qui

solvit Jesum, sayes Saint John in the vul-

1 John
4. 3.

gat. Every spirit that dissolves Jesus, that

embraces not Jesus intirely, all Jesus,

all his truth, and All his, all that suffer

for him, is not of god. Do not say, I will

hold as much of Jesus as shall be necessary,

as much as shall distinguishe me from a

Turke or a Jew; but if I may be better

for parting with some of the rest, why

should I not. Or, I will hold all my selfe,

but let my wife, or my Sonne, or one of

my Sonnes go the other way: as though pro-

testant and papist were two severall rel-

igions, and as you would make one Sonne

a Lawyer, another a Merchant, you will

make one Sonne a papist, another a pro-

testant. Excuse not your own levity, with so

give a dishonor of the prince: when have

you heard, that ever he thanked any Man

for becomming a papist? leave his doors

to him selfe; he doores into his kingdome

and

in your own families. *Omnis spiritus qui* — 1503

soluit Jesum, says <u>Saint John</u> in the vul= — 1504

1 John   gat. Euery spirit that dissolues Iesus, that — 1505

4.3.   embraces not Iesus intirely, all Iesus, — 1506

<u>all his truth, and All his, all</u> that suffer — 1507

for <u>him</u>, is not of god. Do not say I will — 1508

holde as much of Iesus as shall be **necessary**; — 1509

as much, is shall distinguish me from a — 1510

the
Turke or a Iew; but if I may be better — 1511
^

for parting with some of the rest, why — 1512

should I not? <u>Or</u>, I will hold all my selfe, — 1513

but let my wife, or my Sonne, or one of — 1514

my sonns go the other way: as though pro= — 1515

testant and papist, were two seuerall cal= — 1516

lings, and as you would make one Sonne — 1517

a lawyer, another a Merchant, you will — 1518

make one Sonne a papist, another a pro= — 1519

testant. Excuse not your own leuity, with so — 1520

high a dishonor <u>of</u> the prince: when haue — 1521

you heard, that euer he thankd any Man — 1522

for becomming a papist? leaue his dores — 1523

to him selfe; the dores into <u>the kingdome</u> — 1524
and

1504   the Apostle
1507   and *All his, All his Truth,* and *all*
1508   *that Truth*
1510   so much as
1513   Doe not say
1521   to
1524   his kingdome, *The Ports,*

36

and the swords with in the kingdome, the
ports and the prisons. Looke thou seriously
to hine own swords, to hyne owne family,
and keepe them all right there. A theife
that is let out of Newgate, is not therefore
let into thy house. A priest that is let out
of prison, is not therefore sent into thy
house. Still it may be felony to harbor
him, though there were mercy and benignity, to
let him out. Cities are built of families,
and so are Churches too; Every man keepe
his own family, and then every pastor
shall keepe his flock; and so the Church
shalbe free from Schisme, and the State
from sedition, and our Josiah pre=
serued, prophetically, for ours, as he was
historically, this day, from them, in
whose pitts, the breath of our Nostrills,
the anointed of the Lord was taken.
Amen.

and the dores <u>with in</u> the kingdome, the   1525

<u>ports and the prisons</u>. looke thou seriously   1526

to thine own dores, to thyne owne family,   1527

and keepe ~~thou~~ all right there. A theife   1528

that is let out of Newgate, is not therefore   1529

let into thy house. A preist that is let out   1530

of prison, is not therefore <u>sent</u> into thy   1531

<u>house</u>. still it may be felony to harbor   1532

him, though there were **mercy and benignity, to**   1533

<u>let</u> him out.. Cities are built of families,   1534

and so are <u>Churches</u> too; Euery man <u>keepe</u>   1535

his own family, and then euery pastor   1536

shall keepe his flock; and so the Church   1537

shalbe free from *Scisme*, and the state   1538

from ꝑ sedition, and our *Josiah* pre=   1539

serud, prophetically, for euer, as he was   1540

historically, this day, from them, in   1541

whose pitts, the breath of our Nostrills,   1542

the anointed of the lord was taken.   1543

Amen.   1544

1525   in
1526   *prisons;* Let him open and shut his dores, as God shall put into his minde
1531   let
1532   house neither
1533–34 mercy in letting
1535   Chuches ... keeps

Appendix A

Donne's Corrections

CORRECTIONS IN DONNE'S HAND

Definitely Autograph:

Line	Scribe	Donne's Corrections
14	*Johns*	**some** ~~*Johns*~~
82	historical	historically
84	propheticall	prophetically
348	bide there	^**both these** ~~bide there~~
400	now here	**nowhere** ~~now here~~
401	now here	**nowhere** ~~now here~~ ^
544	they implicitly	**came** they implicitly ^
678	reducd	**mou'd** re~~ducd~~ ^
757	affection that	affections ~~that~~ yo **w**
787	~~and~~	**and** ~~and~~ ^
796–7	*vncti Domini, ,*	*vncti Domini,* **the anointed of the Lord, And Spiritus Narium, The Breath of o** [r] **Nostrills.**

802	intreate	**sinuate** in~~treate~~ ^
805	euen the	**in** euen the ^
806	hath	**d** ha~~th~~ ^
826	it, his	**and** it, his
856	it	**y** i~~t~~ ^
918	for them.	**especially** for them. ^
985	wars	**was** ~~wars~~ ^
994	the	**in** ~~the~~ ^
999	now, him	**by** now, him ^
1035	the	**that** ~~the~~ ^
1077	truth	**time** ~~truth~~ ^
1152	that sleeping	that **vision** ~ sleeping
1180	derected	**directed** ~~derected~~ ^
1187	out,was	**and** out, was ^
1337	when as	**ce** when~~as~~ ^
1339–40	is become	is become **Sepher Te =hillim ~~.**

1340	psalms	**psalms** ~~psalms~~ ∧
1350	therefore know	therefore k**we**new ∧
1363	cause	causes
1411	nor	**once** nor ∧
1448	Ambassadors, as	Ambassadors, **is not**, as
1456	even they	even they **who are so** ∧
1509–10	shall be	shall be **necessary; as much,** is
1511	be better	be **the** better ∧
1533–34	were	were **mercy and benignity, to let him out..**

Probably Autograph:

Line Number	Scribe	Correction
Folio 1	Lame	Lame**ntati**
318	was	wa**st**
493	the	th**at**
668	disposed	dis**puted**~~posed~~ ∧
785	the	the **at**
874	curse the	curse **not** the ∧

927	preserud	**ferd** pre~~serud~~
1073	and	**in** ~~and~~
1242	*ducendus*	**i** *d~~u~~cendus* ∧

Possibly Autograph

Line Number	Scribe	Correction
170	*narum*	*narium*
286	a King and	a King: and
327	Dan =	Dan**i**=
345	fault,	fault**;**
451	*reticarum*	*retic**o**rum*
469	*Hæreticarum*	*Hæreticorum*
619	*Quinquenium*	*Quinque**nni**um*
683	certenly	cert**ai**nly
737	speake	speak**s**
739	will	wil**t**
790	*agos*	*ag**is***
879	sae	**E**saye
922	Theophyla	Theophy**lact**
928	Theophlact	Theoph**y**lact
1346	*Derelinquisti*	*Dereli**q**uisti*
1448	by	**E**y
1455	canded	cand**id**

Appendix B

Transcription Details

Transcription Details

4 Cannon: The second "n" appears to be smudged out, and then deleted by a downward stroke through the letter.

14: It is arguable that the underlining strokes which appear on the first three folios of the manuscript are Donne's, by comparison with the stroke through "*Johns*" and under "*Apocalypse*" on this line. This evidence, however, is certainly not conclusive.

25: *Lamentations*: The first letter, "L", appears to be definitely majescule, although the difference between it and other "l's" in the manuscript is one of degree rather than of kind.

42: *Lazarus*: The first letter, "L", is similar to the one at line 25, and has been transcribed as majescule to conform to the scribe's consistent capitalization of proper names.

78 The semicolon after "propheticall" has been superimposed upon a comma.

85 The dot in the semicolon after "againe" doesn't seem to have been made at the same time as the comma. It is far above the line, and in darker ink. It is possible that only the comma was intended here.

90 mourninge: The "e" in this word has been formed above another letter, perhaps an "s".

108 The dot on the semicolon after "*Babilon*" seems to have been added later, in darker ink, possibly by Donne.

111 An=: The "n" is actually smudged out rather than crossed through in the manuscript.

117 *Annointed*: See line 111. The second "n" in this word has been smudged out.

131 tations): The parenthesis was originally a comma, revised to a bracket.

166 The final choice for the punctuation mark after "Kinge" appears

to be a comma, but underneath there are several marks, the most likely of which is a semicolon changed to a comma.

170 *narium*: The "i" of this word has been created by smudging out a letter, and adding a dot. It is possible this correction is Donne's, especially since the scribe's knowledge of Latin is uncertain.

177 yit: The "y" of this word has been added to "it" to form the word. The revision appears to be scribal.

184 the: The letters "at" have been scraped out of the original "that", and the "a" changed to an "e", rather unsuccessfully.

185 the: See line 184.

193 A: It looks as if this word was formed by smudging out a comma and turning it into an unusual descender for this majescule "A".

198 leaue: The original word has been corrected to "leaue" and then crossed out and the word written above more clearly. The hand doesn't seem to be either that of Donne or of the scribe. The "l" and the final "e" forms, for example, are not characteristic of the scribe. However, it is more likely that the correction is scribal than authorial, since the letter forms are not like Donne's other corrections, either in formation or in the colour of ink.

202 Minds: The final "s" in this word is struck through, but in a vertical rather than a horizontal stroke.

237 liuely: An "o" has been changed to an "i", likely by the scribe.

260 king: Although I have transcribed this word as "king," the scribe often dots the last descending stroke in words ending in "ing" so that, literally, the transcription should read "nig" (i.e. "knig"). In all such cases, I have not transcribed this error.

271 that: The word "the" appears to have been changed to "that," likely by the scribe.

271 kinde: A letter, likely an "e", is smudged out to form the word "kind".

278 I am unable to make out the word following "immediat". The last two letters of the word appear to be "nt".

282 The semicolon after "had" could once have been a colon. The comma part of the present semicolon is quite faded.

286 The colon after "king" appears to have been created in revision, possibly by Donne. A second dot has been added to a period.

311 This line is interesting because it contains two of the dots which I have conjectured are used to indicate places where there are correc-

tions to be made or words to be filled in. The dot above "tocratie" in line 311 might indicate that "or such" needs to be added. Similarly the dot after "*noster*" seems to indicate that the Latin words which follow need to be inserted. The scribe does not appear to have left enough room for the three words, however.

319 The inserted clause, "I was," does not appear to be in Donne's hand. Nor does it resemble the scribe's usual corrections. It should be compared with "leaue" on line 198.

327–8 *Dani=el*: The correction to the name "Daniel" is possibly by Donne; the corrector has added the "i" and crossed some letter(s) out at the end of the word.

332 *vsq[ue]*: The transcription expands the manuscript's abbreviation.

341 *Samuel*: The "u" in this word looks as if it was originally a colon for purposes of abbreviation. The word was eventually written in full.

344 theire: The "i" is smudged rather than crossed out.

345 The dot changing a comma to a semicolon appears to have been added later. It is slightly too far above the normal position and in darker ink, possibly changed by Donne.

348 The bottom portion of the semicolon was originally a full stop, changed to a comma.

366 Patriarchs: The stroke on the "c" is dotted, but the letter is clearly a "c".

393 that: This word was originally "it", but was changed to "that". The dot of the "i" remains, and the "t" is the sort commonly used at the end of words in this manuscript.

424 Allegeance: The first letter of this word was originally a miniscule "a" changed to a majescule, probably by the scribe.

425–6M The words in the margin seem to have been corrected, and then ultimately "scalloped" out rather than crossed through.

436 says,: What I have transcribed as a comma after "says" is very faint, and possibly not a mark of punctuation at all.

451 *reticorum*: The "a" in this word has been changed to an "o" by scraping out the tail of the "a". It is uncertain whether the change is scribal or authorial, but is possibly authorial since "Haereticorum" is the correct form of the genetive plural for this word, and, as we have seen, the scribe's Latin is not proficient.

469 *Hæreticorum*: The change from "a" to "o" described in line 451 appears to have been made here once more.

493 th**at**: To form this word the scribal "e" has been changed to "at", probably by Donne.

530 The comma after "himselfe" has been changed from a full stop.

546 *regem*: The last two letters of this word have been corrected from the original, but it is impossible to say what letters they replace.

574 face: The last two letters of this word are unclear. Some other letter(s) have been scraped away, but the intention is clearly the word "face".

577 face: See line 574.

619 *Quinque**nni**um*: Originally, this word was spelled "*Quinquenium*". The doubling of the "n" is possibly Donne's work. This was done by adding two strokes, one after the "e" and before the "n", and one to the other side, to make an "i".

623 The semicolon after "monster" was originally a comma. The dot seems to have been added later.

653 own: A letter, probably an "e", has been scraped away at the end of this word.

654 Ant**i**dote: The first "t" in this word was originally another letter, possibly a "d", scraped out and corrected to a "t".

659 owne: The final "e" is smudged out rather than crossed through.

667 owne: See line 659.

puted

668 dis~~posed~~: This word seems to have been corrected twice, the second correction probably by Donne. It appears that "disposed" was corrected by the scribe to "dispute" and that someone, probably Donne, corrected to the past tense "disputed".

683 cert**ai**nly: It is possible that the correction of the letters "ai" is by Donne.

689 measure: There has been some scraping of the first three letters to produce "measure".

737 speaks: The last letter was created by changing an "e" to an "s", possibly by Donne.

745 Nonresi=: The scribe has changed the initial miniscule "n" to a majescule "N".

772 naturall: Some letter or letters at the end of this word have been scraped out and this spelling inserted.

790 *agis*: Some letter, either an "o" or an "a", has been scraped out and corrected to "i", possibly by Donne.

856 ɨt: The "t" is the scribe's; the "i" corrected to "y" above it is Donne's.

869 seene): The bracket has been formed from what was originally a comma.

907 The dot used to form the semicolon was added later, but it is impossible to attribute.

909 actions: It appears that one letter was changed to "ti", likely by the scribe.

919 ?: A colon has been changed to a question mark.

927 preserud: This correction, likely by Donne, took place in two stages. The first two letters of the correction are in lighter ink, the last two in darker ink, written over.

934 Satir: A letter has been scraped out and corrected to "i"; it is uncertain by whom this was done.

971 It is difficult to construe the marks between "Church" and "who".

1035 ?: A comma has been changed to a semicolon and then to a question mark.

1040 ?: A question mark has been made from a colon.

1052 men: The scribe has attempted to change "man" to "men", but not very successfully.

1078 alterations: The letter has been smudged out rather than crossed through.

1181 the king,: The punctuation mark after the first "king" looks like a period changed to a comma.

1218M The marginal reference has been included and then "scalloped" out.

1231 Something is blotted out after the last syllable of "condemned". Perhaps the scribe initially wrote "condemneth".

1262 taken,: The form of the punctuation mark is confusing, and could also be a semicolon.

1288 There is a comma beneath the ^ after *"Zedechiahs* case".

1289M *Foueis*: The word *"Fouea"* has been corrected by scraping the "a" and inserting "is".

1346 *Derelinquisti*: In this line the "n" has been smudged out, a dot placed over the first stroke on the original "n" to make an "i", and the "q" darkened, possibly by Donne.

1350 knew: The "o" in "know" was changed to "e" by Donne.

1377 There are two marks that can be interpreted as full stops; only the first appears to be intended.

1408 Complexion: The "x" has been formed by smudging out a "t".

1419 The semicolon in this line was originally a comma.

1448 Ey: This word was "by", corrected to "Ey", possibly by Donne.

1451 The dot forming the semi-colon seems to have been added later.

1455 candid: The word appears to have been written originally as "canded"; the "e" has been filled in and dotted to form an "i", possibly by Donne who has added a missing phrase to the line immediately below.